RAGS
THE STORY OF A DOG WHO WENT TO WAR

By
Jack Rohan

Diggory Press would like to thank Gareth Morgan of Castle Hill, NSW, Australia, for his advice on uniforms of military balloonists for our cover design

Originally published 1930, Harper & Bros, New York

Cover Design by Philip John Williams of Staircase Studio

British Library Cataloguing In Publication Data

A Record of This Publication is available from the British Library

ISBN 1905363141

Published by Diggory Press, July 2005, an imprint of
Meadow Books, 35 Stonefield Way, Burgess Hill, West Sussex, RH15 8DW, UK
Email: meadowbooks@hotmail.com
Website www.diggorypress.com

INDEX

RAGS – THE DOG WHO WENT TO WAR

CHAPTER ONE
THE NEW RECRUIT JOINS

BLINDING darkness. Not a gleam anywhere that would act as a beacon, that would give Private Donovan his bearings, as he stood irresolutely in a cul-de-sac of Montmartre. There had been air-raid alarms and Paris was without lights. Donovan was as helpless as a fog-bound ship. In a few hours his outfit—a hand-picked battalion of the First American Division, sent to Paris for the Bastille Day ceremonies—was due to start for the front. For in July, 1918, the Americans were getting ready for the drive that was to end the Great War. It behooved a soldier who prized his good reputation to be on hand when his outfit moved. Donovan's captain was lenient in such little matters as unauthorized absence for a few hours of sightseeing. If the soldier joined his unit before it started, his fault would be dismissed with a tongue-lashing. Absence without leave, when behind the lines A.W.O.L.; the army called it—was the favorite pastime of many of Uncle Sam's best privates. But to be missing when the outfit moved was desertion.

"Might as well have a few people killed by bombs as to have the whole population break its fool neck in the dark," Donovan grumbled as he searched the sky in the hope of finding a star by which he could orient himself. The vault above was merely a leaden cover for the sodden blackness around him. No use to ask directions—he spoke no French.

"Let's get going somewhere," he told himself. "Can't be any worse off than we are. Maybe we'll get a break of luck."

He had picked a few cautious steps when his foot bumped something soft and yielding. There was a low whimper, and then the form entangled itself in his legs, with a subdued but friendly bark. Donovan stooped and felt a warm, shaggy coat. A damp nose sniffed at his hand; a rough little tongue caressed it.

"Friendly little pup," the soldier muttered. "Probably hungry. If I wasn't in such a mess myself, doggie, I'd stake you to a handout, but . . ."

The dog interrupted by standing on its hind legs and placing its forepaws against the soldier. A small tike it was, hardly able to reach above the knees of the strapping Donovan.

"Like me, do you?" inquired the soldier as his ears caught the excited breathing of the dog and the frantic thumping of its tail. "Well, let's see what kind of a man eating mouse-hound you are!"

He struck a match, and barely had caught a glimpse of his new acquaintance when a sharp command came out of the blackness:

"Douse that light!"

Donovan obeyed. As he straightened up, some impulse caused him to gather the dog into his arms. Just why he did it Donovan never was able to explain. He had worries enough, at the moment, without taking a dog to look after. For, although he could not see the person who had ordered the light put out, he knew well enough, from the tone, that he had run afoul of the military police. These army constables accepted no explanations from soldiers found away from their units without passes. Donovan had no pass. Holding the dog closely, he waited the approach of the patrol—a corporal and two privates.

Shaded flashlights were turned on him. His name, that of his unit, and his pass were curtly demanded. No pass? Very well, then; tell it to the lieutenant! Fall in! March! The section was one favored by soldiers seeing the sights, whether with passes or without. So a police post had been placed in the heart of it. Donovan had become lost within a block of it, so the march was short. His vision was blurred for a moment as he stepped from the outside pitchiness into the light of the guard-room, dim though it was. He could think of no satisfactory repartee for the sally of a sergeant who, noticing the shaggy burden in his arms, remarked:

"This guy's bringin' in a bunch of rags, so he'll have a pillow in the jail-house!"

When Donovan's vision cleared, he glanced down at the dog. It dawned on him that the sergeant was right—the curled-up puppy looked pretty much like a bundle of old olive-drab uniforms. The discovery gave him an inspiration—an explanation of his absence from his unit without a pass—as he studied the lieutenant, a pleasant-faced young chap with whom one might be able to reason.

"Did you lose your pass, Private Donovan?" the officer asked in a tone not unkindly.

"No, sir," Donovan replied, his heart and brain racing in hopeful excitement as his alibi idea began to develop. "There wasn't time to get a pass, sir. The outfit was getting ready to move, and I had to work fast or we'd have had to leave him behind."

"Leave who behind?"

"Our mascot, sir. The dog here. He followed some of the men who had leave, and they came back without him. I was about the only one who didn't have immediate duty. So I hustled out to look for him without stopping to get a pass."

"Had quite a search, I presume?"

6

"Ye"s, sir. And just after I found him the lights went out and I couldn't get my bearings."

"H'm! Company mascot, I suppose?" The lieutenant's hand moved toward a telephone. Donovan guessed he was going to call up the company and break the news that the mascot had been found. So Private Donovan did what the army calls "fast thinking."

"Not the company mascot, sir," he explained. "He's sort of mascot to the whole First Division. He hangs out with one company for a while, and then goes with another. Sometimes he'll stay around with the generals, and then, again, he'll make himself at home with the cook's police. You see, sir, if we lost him, we'd have the whole division on our neck!"

"H'm, I see. What kind of dog is he?" Donovan didn't have the least idea, but he had heard somewhere that a shaggy coat usually marked one of the Scotch or Irish breeds, so he hazarded a guess:

"Highland terrier, sir."

"And his name?"

"Rags, sir," Donovan replied without the slightest hesitation, mentally blessing the jesting sergeant who had supplied the idea.

"Put him down."

Donovan obeyed. The dog snuggled close to his feet, and gazed inquiringly from Donovan to the officer, and from the officer to the military-police detail. There was no partisanship in his glance. It was plain that he was devoted to Donovan. But these folk had a friendly scent and if they wanted to develop an acquaintance with him, the dog was willing. His tail beat a tattoo on the floor.

"Come here, Rags!" the officer commanded.

Donovan's heart sank. He suspected that the dog understood only French, which was, indeed, the fact. The canine waif had no idea of the meaning of the officer's words. But he gathered from the tone and attitude—and from a pressure of Donovan's foot—what was wanted. Assuming a pose resembling "attention," he advanced slowly and with a certain dignity. Then he sat up, with his front paws uplifted and his keen little face wearing a quizzical expression so noticeable in the terrier breeds.

"Highland terrier, eh!" the officer remarked. "Well, I guess he has as much claim to that as to several other distinguished lines of ancestry. If he has the good points of all of 'em he ought to be a whale of a dog. Know the name of the place where your outfit is billeted?"

Donovan gave the information snappily, suppressing, with effort, a

7

sigh of relief. It looked as if the dog had wangled him out of a jam.

"Have you any money?" the officer inquired, explaining that if Donovan could hire a cab to take himself and a guide to the billets of his unit and bring back the guide to the police post, a man would be assigned to return him to his outfit. Donovan thanked his stars he had cash for the required transportation. With a military-police sergeant who knew Paris inside out, Donovan and the dog rode toward the billet of the First Division group. The terrier utilized the travel time to establish friendly relations with the cynical straw-boss of the army constabulary.

"The little mutt ain't just a division dog," the sergeant confided to Donovan. "He's a friend o' the whole A.E.F."

And he continued to scratch the dog's back and neck in comradely fashion, until a sharp challenge brought the ride to an end.

Donovan had approached the billets with some misgivings. If he should blunder on a strange unit, or if an unfriendly sentry should be on post, the fiction of restoring the division mascot might be exposed. In such a contingency the military-police sergeant might feel bound to return to his commanding officer and report— taking Donovan with him. Donovan glowed with relief when he recognized the challenging voice. It belonged to one of his best friends, "Midget" Slattery, a quick-witted Irishman. Donovan answered promptly, but not loudly:

"Private Donovan—with the division mascot!"

"Private Donovan—with the division mascot" was ordered to advance for recognition, which was enough for the guide, who grunted an order to the cabman and was on his way before Slattery's shaded flashlight had picked out Donovan.

"Where'd you get the pup?" the sentry inquired in a stage whisper, lest the corporal of the guard hear.

"Up Montmartre way," Donovan whispered in reply, and explained, briefly, what had occurred. "I'm goin' to make him our mascot," he added.

"Well, on your way," Slattery advised. "I didn't see you come in."

The dog moved restlessly in Donovan's arms. There was the same friendly something about this sentry that his psychic nose had detected about the other men who had accosted his friend. He wanted to get acquainted with Slattery. A homeless dog, in a land that seemed strangely indifferent to the fate of man's canine friends, should know as many of these agreeable folk as possible—even though they spoke in a strange tongue. So he appeared to reason. He gave just the suggestion of a bark—promptly squelched by Donovan.

8

"Hush up, puppy," the soldier warned, "or you'll be talking us into trouble."

From the tone, and the kindly, yet urgent pressure of the big soldier's arms, the dog understood that, for some reason, silence was desired. He scarcely breathed.

"Smart little pooch," Slattery whispered.

"You bet you," Donovan agreed, and began feeling his way toward his billet with a murmured, "So long, and thanks," to his friend.

Being a Signal Corps specialist, Donovan had not been concerned much with the outfit's preparations for moving beyond making his own pack. And in the hustle and bustle of getting the crack battalion on its way his absence had passed unnoticed. So he kept his own counsel and slipped into the mess kitchen as nonchalantly as if he had just stepped out of it. In the none too bright light he examined his canine recruit. The little fellow was weak from hunger—but game. His coat, normally ragged and shaggy, was tangled and snarled from foraging—probably futilely— through the streets and alleys of Paris. But there was a brave gleam in his eyes, and his tail thumped a sort quick-step as he sat and looked Donovan over.

The mess sergeant listened to Donovan's story, spoke a few words to the dog, noticed his puzzled air, and then tried him out in French. There was immediate response, in eloquent barking, and increased vibration of tail. Food was prepared and placed on the floor. But the dog seemed to have decided to show that he was well mannered. He would not eat until invited—and he didn't understand the English words. Half famished though he was, he was taking no chances of offending these new friends. He felt certain they were going to feed him, but he deemed it politic to have them tell him so in a language he understood. He waited, stiff and tense, panting his friendliness.

The sergeant, speaking French, told him to eat. When the dog had taken a few morsels the bilingual mess chief lifted the dish from the floor, repeated the English words several times, set the dish down, and told the dog first in French and then in English that the food was for him. And to make it perfectly plain he pushed the terrier's nose into the dish as he gave the final English translation. From that minute on, nobody ever had to translate "Come an' get it!" for Rags—Rags being the name Donovan gave him, formally and officially, as he ate his initial Rookie ration with the First Division, A. E. F.

9

CHAPTER TWO
AND SO TO WAR!

RAGS, finishing his first A. E. F. meal, was putting a final polish on his dish when a soldier hurried in and spoke to Donovan.

"Say, where have you been hiding?" he demanded, "I've hunted all over the place for you. The cap'n wants to see you right away."

"What's he want?" Donovan inquired, nervously wondering if, after all, his unauthorized absence had been discovered and he was in for a session with the captain, who was a brilliant conversationlist, to put it mildly, pointing out a soldier's shortcomings.

"I didn't think to inquire," the other retorted, ironically. "I suppose he wants to kiss you on both cheeks and pin a medal on you! Come to think of it, he did say something about being fed up on his job and wantin' you to take his place, if you'd be so kind!"

"Well," growled Donovan, nettled at the other's sarcasm and worried lest the captain had discovered his absense, "if I was runnin' the outfit, I know one ribbon clerk that'd be back doin' light housekeepin' for the cook's police, instead o' gettin' his feet tangled up in signal wires."

With that he stamped out of the door, Rags following. He entered the captain's quarters with some misgiving, but a glance at the officer's face reassured him. There were no storm signals. Whatever the "skipper" wanted, it had nothing to do with a reprimand.

"Took long enough to find you," the captain commented, "but in this infernal blackness a man can't find his own feet. Break yourself out a set of sergeant's chevrons. I'm going up to division supply. You're coming with me—as a sergeant!"

"Thank you, sir," said Donovan, snapping to attention. "When do I start?"

"You've started. And don't thank me. Thank yourself. You're a darned good signalman, Donovan. Where'd you get the funny pup?"

"I didn't get him, sir. He got me. Just sort of adopted me, I guess. Stumbled over him in the dark, and found I'd collected me a mascot."

Donovan hoped the captain wouldn't ask where he'd stumbled over Rags. He hated to lie—and he was not anxious to make admissions that might cost him his chevrons before he had them sewed on his blouse. The officer sought no particulars, but explained the new assignment. It was an emergency trouble-shooting detail—one of those odd jobs that is always dropping into the laps of the signal and engineering groups of every military organization in the world. He revealed that most of the Bastille Day battalion of the First Division was already on its way back to the front, that he and Donovan were to follow as rapidly as possible, make contact with division headquarters, and organize a special service for the establishment of communications which broke down under stress of battle.

When the officer finished talking, Rags sat down in front of him. The dog liked this captain, in spite of his brusque mannerisms. Rags knew he had found another friend when the officer tweaked his ears and with the unerring accuracy of a man who understood dogs.

"Great little pup," he said to Rags. "Want to join the army, do you?"

Rags, of course, didn't understand. The captain noticed his blank expression and repeated the remark in French. The terrier's tail got into action at once and he gave a bark—a more forceful sound than he had been able to manage when Donovan found him, hungry in the blackness of Montmartre.

"So?" said the captain. "You're a Frog, are you? Stick around, Doggie, and we'll make a good Massachusetts republican out of you yet."

"May I Keep the dog, sir?" Donovan asked.

"Certainly. He's a bright little chap. The Scotch and Irish breeds generally are. He's got some of both, I'd say—no pure-bred, certainly. But some of the best dogs, like some of the best folks, have a lot of mixed ancestry."

Rags followed the new sergeant to the latter's billet and, finding a comfortable corner, decided it was high time for a nap. But he had scarcely stretched himself out when Donovan began making up a pack and told him:

"If you're going to stick with the party, Rags, you'll have to snap out of it!"

The meaning, of course, would have been obvious to a less intelligent dog than Rags, who trotted after Donovan as the sergeant, pack on back, proceeded to where a number of big motor-trucks were standing, not far from the building where Rags had met the friendly captain. There were other soldiers there, too. Donovan lifted Rags to one of the trucks and then climbed aboard himself. The other men were all pleasant and friendly, although one or two of them asked Rags to do foolish things, such as jumping through their hands. Rags couldn't understand what they wanted at first, but the tone in which they spoke, and their gestures, soon enlightened him as to what "jump" meant. He merely turned his back on these playful persons and snuggled close to

Donovan.

When the trucks began to move, Rags found a comfortable place to sleep on a pile of packs on the floor. He didn't know where he was going, and he didn't particularly care. The trucks rumbled over the roads in the general direction of Soissons. Rags's slumbers were disturbed by a strange booming. As the truck train proceeded the sound became clearer. When it became almost continuous Rags appeared to feel something was amiss. He sat up nervously and sniffed around among the soldiers until his nose rested against Donovan.

"Just a little strafing, Doggie," the sergeant told him, "It's hard on your nerves at first, but you'll get used to it. We all had to."

Rags, of course, wouldn't have understood the words, even had he known English. But he gathered from Donovan's tone that there was nothing to worry about, so he went back to sleep. When he awakened again day was breaking, and his nose told him that there were of thousands of these friendly-scented, kindly folk on all sides of him, apparently coming from many directions and intent on a common goal.

He acted as if he wanted to quit the truck and go around and make some new friends. But his good sense him to stick to the pal he knew— Donovan— o he sat on the truck and watched the American horde tramping forward—to what was to be the battle of Soissons. As the gray of the dawn became lighter, the trucks moved into a patch of timber and parked. Rags noticed that as the daylight heightened the roads became comparatively deserted. The infantry who had been marching, the artillerymen who had been sweating, pushing and hauling their guns through the mud, had all disappeared. Just as Rags's group had sought shelter in the woods, these others secreted themselves in timber or in clumps of ruins well off the road.

The crashing and thundering became more intense. Rags observed that every now and then fragments of ground would fly high in the air. He discovered that a certain noise could be heard approaching before the great blast and the geyser of earth came. The dog also noticed that Sergeant Donovan and his other friends dropped prone when they heard the sound. So, Rags, too, got the trick of lying as close to the ground as his little body could get. He didn't know why, probably, but he apparently understood there was some good reason why everyone was doing it. He hoped, though—his whole attitude made that plain—that this business of ground flying up into the air would come to an end. But, instead, it became more violent. His friends covered their faces with strange contrivances that made them look like monsters with great long noses. Donovan rigged up a contraption and placed it over Rags's head. It made breathing difficult and was hot and uncomfortable—a nuisance. Rags found he could see through it only now and then, as the glass windows in it kept slipping around out of his line of vision, and it made it impossible for him to use his sense of smell. He tried to get it off, but couldn't.

He was relieved when the truck train suddenly started to move, especially since the spouting and churning of the ground was getting closer. He hoped things would get quieter, that perhaps his friends were going back whence they came. But he was in for a disappointment. The trucks were moving because the enemy artillery had located them. Rags was getting his baptism of fire at the opening of the drive toward Fere-en-Tardenois and Soissons.

CHAPTER THREE
THE PATH OF GLORY

DONOVAN surveyed his job—the task of keeping wire connections between advancing infantry and artillery—and decided that where he was going would be no place for Rags. So the sergeant took the dog on an "A. W. O. L." expedition back to division headquarters and placed him in the care of a sergeant-major. But Rags had a mind of his own, and while Donovan was explaining the necessity for leaving him behind he jumped through a window, unobserved, and waited outside.

Furtively he followed the sergeant, taking no chances of revealing himself until he felt they were far enough from headquarters to make it reasonably certain Donovan would not take him back. It was not until Donovan caught up with the Seventh Field Artillery in Couvres Ravine that Rags deemed it expedient to appear. Then he timidly nuzzled the sergeant's heels. Donovan chuckled and scratched the dog's neck affectionately.

"So you're bound to stick with me?" he observed. "If that's the way you feel about it we'll go through this business together. Come on."

Rags was beginning to understand words as well as tones and gestures. He already had learned that "come on" meant he was wanted. He contentedly fell in beside Donovan as the sergeant moved about, cutting in on new wire, feeling his way along another or stringing a new line to complete some broken circuit. Shell were dropping here and there in desultory fashion, but the fire had not yet reached the stage that made the terrain a spouting caldron. Donovan knew that when the battle was going full blast many of his carefully-placed lines would be torn to fragments, that communications would break down, and that the fate of advanced infantry in many a crisis would depend on the ability of the runners to get through.

Rags, the sergeant had noticed, did not take kindly to learning tricks. But he judged that if the terrier could be taught there was some good reason for carrying messages he might, in a pinch, get one through. He took advantage of a comparative lull to explain the duties of a runner to Rags. With amazing patience he made the dog understand what was wanted. He set the example by carrying papers himself. He called the dog to him after another soldier had placed a folded newspaper in Rags's teeth. Eventually he taught Rags that when a paper was given to him he was to bring it to Donovan, and that when Donovan placed a paper in

Rags's teeth and said "Go find," the dog was to carry it toward the guns until he found some one who would take it from him.

While Rags's education proceeded the enemy fire was increasing. But the dog paid little attention to it except for hugging the ground when his ear caught the sound of a shell that was likely to land close by. Only when gas began falling and Donovan clapped the mask on him did the terrier appear uneasy. The thing was uncomfortable and he did his best to get it off.

There were times when Donovan was too busy to remove the mask for Rags, and the terrier developed the habit of appealing to other soldiers. If none appeared, he would scurry back toward the artillery and apply to the cannoneers. At Laversine—the night of, July 17th-18th —he was seeking riddance of the gas mask, and got his first close-up of the effect of shell-fire on men. A pleasant-voiced private named Welch had removed the mask for Rags, scratched the dog's head, fed him, and given him a drink when the shell came.

Rags heard the gasping whine that he had learned would be followed by a crash and spouting of ground. He rolled into a hole. A jarring explosion spattered him with dirt. He lay quiet for a minute and then peeped over the edge of his shelter. Probably it was the first time the dog realized why Donovan and his friends took cover or hugged the ground when they heard the sound that warned of a coming shell. The things certainly were burdened with mischief. But he did not grasp the full extent of the evil until he saw Private Welch writhing on the ground.

Rag's nose, as soon as the pungent smell of the powder fumes cleared a little, told him his friend was bleeding. Instinctively he knew it was not good for people to bleed. He scrambled out of his hole and went to the side of Private Welch. The soldier was lying motionless. The dog's instinct told him the man was still alive and he licked Welch's face and outstretched hands, still vibrant from the shock of pain. Finding this did no good, he looked around for Donovan, and failing to find him, he turned his attention to the soldiers who were working the guns and pranced and barked until a couple of them accompanied him to the spot where Welch lay.

The gunners placed the wounded man on a blanket and poured something out of a bottle into his wounds. Then they shook their heads dubiously, muttered something about "going west," and returned to their work at the guns. Rags was surprised at the scant attention given Private Welch. There were many things about war a dog could not understand. He was obviously more at ease when, after an interval, some men came along, lifted the wounded man on to a stretcher and carried him away. Rags knew, somehow, that these folk would do the best they could for the wounded soldier, so he set out to meet Donovan.

The sergeant, heading back toward the battery, scolded Rags for getting rid of his gas mask, and went in search of it. He found it behind the guns, where Private Welch had dropped it before being hit, and lectured the terrier at length on the necessity of keeping the mask. The shell-fire was growing more intense minute by minute. Frequently now Rags saw men fall and lie still. He knew they would never move or speak again. With the earth spouting up on all sides Rags and Donovan hopped from shell hole to shell hole. The enemy's heavy artillery was pounding the sector, and the American guns, in full cry, were answering. The racket was deafening. But Rags's ear distinguished the various sounds. By some special canine sense he could catch the approach of a shell before the soldiers heard it. It became the habit of Donovan—and any others who were about—to watch Rags and take cover at his warning. The dog always gave a growling little bark before ducking to safety. By the night of July 19th Rags was a thoroughly fire-seasoned veteran.

The morning of the 20th dawned on a desperate struggle for possession of the Paris-Soissons road, to which the Second Brigade of the First Division was hanging by its teeth, with the enemy throwing everything he had in an effort to make it let go. Donovan's detail was trying frantically to keep communications open behind the command post of the Twenty-eighth Infantry, whose advanced units had taken a terrible mauling. Wires were mashed and tangled as fast as they were put down. Runners were dropping like bowling-pins. As the morning dragged on the regimental command became insistent in a demand for its advanced troops. The wires had been out for hours. Donovan struggled hopelessly with the many breaks.

Rags brought the information for which the colonel was clamoring. He had taken it upon himself to make use of the training Donovan had given him and scurried up to the sergeant with a folded note in his mouth. Donovan opened it and read:

"I have forty-two men, mixed, healthy, and wounded. We have advanced to the road, but can go no farther. Most of the men are from the Twenty-sixth Infantry. I am the only officer. Machine-guns at our rear, front, right and left. Send infantry officer to take command. I need machine gun ammunition."

The message bore the signature of a second lieutenant, the commander of the troops headquarters had been so anxious to locate.

16

Donovan relayed it over the phone and then set about finding the runner. The man had been cut down by a shell. He never knew what had killed him.

Rags, apparently, had found the paper and, remembering that Donovan liked to have papers brought to him, had picked it up and delivered it. By way of reward Donovan took Rags into a shell hole, made one of the speeches of commendation he knew pleased the dog, and gave him food and water. Realizing that he had done well, Rags began watching for runners who got caught in the fire.

In the two succeeding days through which the battle raged, Donovan began to regard Rags as his most useful helper, and he watched sharply to make sure some of the troops who were moving in to relieve the First Division did not steal his pal away from him.

Rags displayed keen interest in the newcomers. They were big strapping fellows, and were dressed as the dog never had seen men dressed before. Their gaily-colored top clothes were in striking contrast with the olive drab of the Americans, and instead of breeches or trousers they wore short skirts that displayed their powerful knotted knees. They were friendly enough toward Rags and called him a "bonnie wee doggie."

Rags understood the "doggie," but most of what the Scots said was strange to him. Rags had no memory of the dialect of his Highland ancestors. The Scots would have welcomed the terrier as a mascot, but as soon as Rags found that Donovan and the First Division were headed for the rear, he wasted no time making friends among the Highlanders. The strain of the prolonged battle had told on Rags. Like the rest of the First Division, he needed a rest.

CHAPTER FOUR
RAGS MEETS HIS GENERAL

WHILE Rags was resting with the First Division in the Dammartin area he expanded his knowledge of English, improved his message-carrying technique, and, under the patient tutelage of Donovan, learned something of the customs and courtesies, so called, of the service. The sergeant taught him a sort of salute, and it became the terrier's practice, when he saw the soldiers saluting, to sit back on his haunches and lift his right paw toward his eye. The training did not deter him from making a thorough general inspection of the whole division, with particular attention to the mess arrangements of the engineers, signal corps, artillery, infantry, and special service. Donovan made no attempt to curtail Rags's wanderings. The sergeant took the view that Rags regarded him as a friend, that the canny little terrier never would recognize anyone as a master.

On one of his tours of inspection Rags noticed a group of soldiers watching a sergeant, who was teaching them the art of grenade throwing. Rags stopped to watch. One suspects he wondered if the sergeant was playing a "throw and fetch" game with the soldiers. Attempts had been made by many members of the First Division to interest Rags in that game. But all failed. When a stick or ball was tossed and Rags was told to "Go fetch!" he merely turned his back on the playful soldier and stalked away. One got the impression that Rags felt it beneath the dignity of a dog who had been under fire to play games. Rags pricked up his ears as the sergeant began to talk. The man was explaining that, having demonstrated with dummy grenades, he would throw the real thing.

As the lethal "egg" left the sergeant's hand, a big handsome collie, mascot of a machine-gun company, came along, saw the grenade flying through space, and dashed toward it. The collie liked to play Only a masterly flying tackle by the instructor saved that collie. The sergeant dived for the dog and, flinging both arms around its neck, forced it close to the ground as the grenade exploded some twenty feet away, showering dog and soldier with dirt and shrapnel splinters. Rags stood watching with the air of one who pities the stupidity of the world in general. He strolled over to the frightened collie, nuzzled it as if whispering consolation, and then trotted away for a tour of inspection of division headquarters.

As Rags neared the headquarters he passed a careless-looking soldier shambling along, with the top two buttons of his blouse unfastened. A little farther on he met a solitary officer, pacing along meditatively— General Charles P. Summerall, the division commander. Rags had seen him before, but never had managed to strike up an acquaintance. There is little doubt, in view of the peculiar psychic sense so strongly developed in terriers, that Rags knew the general was a person of importance and had sensed on previous occasions the unrest among officers when General Summerall came around inspecting their commands. Probably the dog was sometimes reminded, by the general's snapping criticisms of incompetence, of certain unfriendly folk of his puppy days in Paris who generally followed their abuse of Rags by an attempt to kick him. Rags never had seen the general try to kick anybody, but there was a certain hopeful expectancy in his manner as the general hailed the slovenly soldier Rags had passed a few moments before. The man came out of his reverie, advanced to within a few paces of the general, and saluted.

"What's the matter, young man?" the commander inquired. "Haven't you joined the army yet?"

"Yes, sir. But I just came into the camp and I was tired. I was thinking about the folks back home and I didn't see the general."

"I'm not talking about your failure to salute. I'm talking about this," grasping the man's blouse and buttoning the lower button, "and this," fastening the top one and pulling the jacket smooth with a smart rug. "Don't you realize that if General Pershing saw my men running around looking as sloppy as you he'd probably court-martial me?"

The soldier flushed and stammered an apology. The general smiled. But his voice was crisp when he spoke:

"All right. Run along. Keep your chin up. And you'd better not fail to see any second lieutenants, unless you want your ears burned!"

The man moved on after saluting with a snap. Rags trotted over in front of the general, sat up, and gave his own version of the ancient military greeting. The general didn't notice him until Rags barked sharply—a bark that was really a sort of apologetic half-cough.

"Hello!" said the general. "You look as if you were trying to salute. What can we do for you?"

Rags barked again and beat a tattoo with his tail. The general reached down and scratched the terrier's neck and back. Then he stepped past the dog, intent on his own thoughts. Rags took the hint. The general had something on his mind. The terrier dropped behind and followed the general until the latter disappeared into his quarters. Then Rags set out to discover what sort of mess arrangements this vibrant personage had. He found the kitchen without difficulty. The mess sergeant and the cooks were glad to see him, but dogs were not welcome around the cooking arrangements of division commanders. Rags appeared to sense that the kitchen crew were friendly, but that at the same time these men were getting ready to put him out. He stood in the middle of the room with an air of indecision. An officer entered and noticed him.

"He just came in," the mess sergeant explained. "We were getting ready to put him out."

"Oh, don't do that," the officer laughed as he strolled over and scratched the dog's head. "He's a friend of the general's. I saw them conferring outside a few minutes ago. It'll be all right to feed him."

Rags, who had been listening intently, watching the faces of the men and sniffing audibly, settled down in a corner and waited until they brought him a pork chop, some bread soaked in gravy, and a bowl of water. He decided he might stay.

The mess sergeant remarked to the cook, "I think the little pooch will bring us luck."

"Yeah," the cook retorted. "He's a smart little fellow an' he'll prob'ly stick with us. He knows good chow when he gets it."

"Who's pinnin' medals on you?" spoke up one of the cook's police detail.

"Not you," growled the sergeant. "You couldn't pin nothin' on yourself—'cept a row o' dishrags; an' start using some of 'em."

Rags appeared interested mainly in the lingering flavor of the gravy. He was polishing his dishes as no kitchen police detail ever did. The sergeant watched him with a sort of awe.

"Guess we've got us a dawg mascot," he opined, and went away.

So did Rags. Having feasted, and probably, canny tike that he was, made a mental note that the general's kitchen was a good place to drop into, he set out to hunt up Donovan.

Donovan was looking for Rags at about the same time. Knowing the dog's habits, he was going from mess to mess, trying to find him. Donovan had received orders to move, and he wasn't leaving Rags behind if he could help it. It was an army version of a couple of friends searching for each other and moving so rapidly that one or the other always got that time-honored bulletin, "He's been here, but he left about five minutes ago." How long the search might have continued is anybody's guess. But Rags saw a cat.

The cat arched its back and spat at him. Rags dashed for the cat. The cat miaowed, spat, hissed, and ran. Rags a reasonably experienced hand at the game of chasing nine lives, barked. Then things began to happen. This particular cat had wandered into the area homeless and friendless, but had managed to get himself under the protection of an officer known to his comrades as "Teddy." Besides being voted "one swell soldier" by all of his subordinates and superiors, the officer was the son of a former President of the United States and had a lot of friends. There was a grand rally to rescue his cat. The officers and soldiers in the immediate vicinity armed themselves with sticks and stones and set out to hamper Rags's pursuit of the cat. But the cat and dog were moving so rapidly that nothing short of a machine-gun barrage could have stopped either of them. The rescue squad did its best. Donovan, prowling through a mess-hall near by, heard the racket and hurried to see what it was all about. By the time he arrived the cat had climbed a stub of telephone pole and was spitting defiance at the dog. The terrier was indicating that he wished he'd been born a lineman, but he seemed to realize there was no sense in wasting any more time on the cat, so when he heard Donovan call he trotted meekly away from the foot of the pole. The cat's friends, seeing their charge safe and the terrier moving away, went back to their pinochle and African-domino games.

Donovan loaded Rags into the side-car of a motorcycle and, as was his habit, talked to the dog.

"Cut out chasing staff colonel's cats," he advised,' "You'll have to do it if you're trailing with me."

Rags barked and thumped the bottom of the side-car with his tail as if to say he knew they were going somewhere and was glad of it.

"Yeah," Donovan remarked, understandingly, "we're heading up Sazarais way. Some colored folks from Morocco need a little vacation. We're going to keep books for 'em while they see gay Paree. They say it's a quiet sector, but I'll bet you a good mutton bone, Rags, that is it is they don't leave us there long."

Rags again wagged his tail understandingly and settled against Donovan's feet for a nap.

Next morning, the 12th of August, he awakened to find himself in the midst of First Division troops going the same way he was going, and strange-looking black folk moving in the opposite direction, to the rear.

Rags catching a first scent of the blacks—they were Moroccans—turned up his nose and barked angrily. He made it plain he did not like them, although they talked to him pleasantly enough, even offered him some of their scanty rations and invited him to come with them.

Donovan was worried lest these dark warriors—as strange to him as

21

they were to Rags—should steal his canine friend. But he acquired a certain sense of security as he realized that Rags did not favor them and that the dog did not understand their language even when they interlarded their remarks with a fair percentage of their own conception of French. But his suspicions returned when, for the third time, he found a strapping black sergeant regaling Rags with a basin of tinned milk. Donovan decided that, ally or no ally, he was not letting any Morocco noncom lure Rags from him. He shouted to one of his squad.

"Bill, you speak Frog," the sergeant snapped. "Find some Frenchy that speaks this Moroccan lingo and have 'im tell this bird that if he tries to swipe Rags I'll have his hide for a shelter half!"

"Dat's all right, Mistuh Sah-gent," the giant Negro spoke up. "You-all doan' need no interpertuh. Ah's a Yankee like youahse'f, an' ah has no perdispositions to steal youah dawg. Ah's just doin' him a favoh, as one 'Merican citizen to anothah!"

Donovan was flabbergasted for a moment. But the big Negro continued, imperturbably, to explain that he was a sailor, spoke many languages after a fashion, and had joined the Moroccan division to "see the show." He told how his experiences in an American colored regiment had given him prestige with the French officers.

"Ah's a big man with mah officahs," he explained, "These heah ig'orant Morocco niggahs ain't been no place an' ain't seen nothin'. Ah's f'om Alabam', an' daown theah ah's just anothah niggah. But with thest i folks ah's somebody. You-all doan' need to worry abaut youah dawg."

Donovan accepted the Moroccan sergeant's word at its face value, but he kept a watchful eye on Rags, nevertheless. He felt reasonably certain that nobody could lure Rags from the First Division—but why take chances?

"You guys watch Rags," he ordered his men. "Nobody's goin' to coax him away, for he wouldn't go; but I knew an Igorote once that stole General Lawton's dog right out o' the general's tent. I ain't taking no risks."

When the relief was completed, Donovan became busy patching lines that had been neglected by the signal troops supporting the Moroccans. It was a quiet sector and the French signalmen felt no great urge to exert themselves unduly. There was, of course, the daily strafing hour—that came off as regularly as monastery prayers—but it didn't mean anything. Nevertheless, Donovan and his crew held the view that one might need those lines some day. So they ranged far afield patching and replacing wire. Besides, Donovan figured, it gave him a chance to perfect Rags in the business of getting through to the artillery, in a major emergency.

There were times when Rags became bored with watching Donovan and his aids working on the wires, and with carrying papers to the guns when nothing in particular appeared to happen. But the terrier learned the battery locations so well that if, after a few hours of separation from Donovan, he was unable to find the sergeant where he had left him, he would gallop to the positions of the Seventh Field Artillery, apparently knowing that sooner or later Donovan would turn up there.

It was on August 12th that he was thus seeking Donovan, only to find the artillery getting ready to move. The sergeant did not appear. But Rags stuck with the guns and rode the caissons as they bumped over the roads to go into the rest area at Vaucouleurs. He was compelled to ride them again after five days, for the orders to move had come through with such urgency that the sergeant had no time to hunt up Rags. The terrier was forced to fend for himself as the First Division moved up for the San Mihiel push, with Donovan far in the advance and Rags and the artillery bringing up the rear.

CHAPTER FIVE
BALLOONISTS AND BATTLE

SOLDIERS making a forced march have scant time to care for the needs of a dog. There was no halting for rations as the caisson on which Rags was riding hopped and slide over the shell-torn roads. Rags was hungry. At every crossroad he would stand stiffly atop the ammunition-box and scan the surrounding soldiery, looking for Donovan. Troops of all arms were moving forward. The congestion was greater than at Soissons. Back of Beaumont the artillery pulled to one side to pass some signal-corps trucks. Donovan, standing beside one of them, called to Rags. The terrier barked a greeting and then jumped off the caisson to join his friend. On the ground he found himself in imminent danger of being stepped on by the marching men and horses, or run over by the wheels of the artillery and trucks. Unable to make progress against the current of the march, Rags drifted with it as he wormed his way to the outer edge of the column and got off the road. By the time he had detoured back to where he had sighted Donovan, the sergeant had gone elsewhere. Rags picked up the trail readily, and followed it across the fields to a clump of woods.

Donovan had passed through the wood, but Rags, getting his first close-up of a captive balloon, paused to inspect it. The big gas-bag, anchored to a truck, was pulled well below the tree-tops. There were a number of soldiers around the place, but Rags paid no attention to them. The balloon's basket interested him, probably because he had often found food in contraptions similar, although considerably smaller. He jumped up on the truck and from the truck to a sort of shelf on the rim of the basket. Inside, a couple of observers squatted. Rags sniffed at them and they spoke to him pleasantly, Satisfied, he dropped in with them.

"No, no!" one of the men said. "This is no place for you, puppy!"

"Aw, let him come, Bill," the other protested. "The little pooch may bring us luck."

"Suppose we get shot down—as we probably will! I don't want to have to hide my head from the soldier that owns that dog."

"We'll take him with us when we go overboard. I've been over so often now that I could carry an elephant down."

"Yeah! But suppose the gent who breaks up our party gets a notion to see how good a wing shot he is?"

"Shucks! Those guys aren't such bad sports. They're not going to knock off a gent that's lugging a dog down with him. The pup's good life insurance, if you ask me!"

"Well, it's okay by me. He acts hungry. I'll donate one of these sandwiches if you'll kick in with another. Guess he's thirsty, too. He'll have to drink out of a tin hat."

The man leaned over the side of the balloon car and called to a soldier.

"Let's take your bone kettle for a minute, Mike. We're mixing a Croton cocktail for a dog."

Mike flung his steel helmet to them and they filled it with water. Rags drank, ate the sandwiches, which they obligingly broke up for him, and drank again. They tossed the helmet back to its owner. The balloon began to move. As it shot upward, swaying on the end of its Cable, Rags stood nervously tense in the center of the car. The observers talked to the dog in low, reassuring tones, stroked his head, and urged him to lie down. He curled up and went to sleep, lulled by the sway of the balloon and the voices of his companions into telephones connected with the ground.

The roar and rattle of bursting shell, so near that the concussion jarred the basket, awakened him. Other burst came in quick succession and Rags flattened himself on the floor. But when the observers did not do likewise, Rags abandoned his battle-taught safety measures and tried to peer over the car rim to see what they were watching. He was too small to reach it and there was so little room in the car that his leap for the rim fell short—a lucky thing for Rags. No four-footed creature could have balanced itself on that jerking, swaying, basket edge. The observers were watching an enemy airplane, which was trying to get at the balloon through the anti-aircraft fire that had awakened Rags.

"How come our own Air never can keep these babies from getting through?" Bill inquired, querulously.

"Ask me an easy one. Why weren't guys like us born with wings?"

"That Fokker's tryin' to deliver a couple o' sets to us, with harps to match. And if . . ."

"Look!" the other interrupted. "Do you see what I see? There's the movement the Old Man wanted to know about!"

Both men gazed in silence through their glasses for a moment, then Bill spoke into the telephone. He listened and again talked into the mouthpiece. Then he shouted and dropped the thing with a gesture of disgust.

"Gone blooey!" he complained. "And us with the dope we were sent up to get. Say, there's something else going on, too. See that dust. They're moving artillery."

Both men began writing rapidly in notebooks, repeating to each other cryptic letters and numerals which they checked on a map. The firing was continuous and the enemy flyer was twisting and dodging, but persistently circling. Each manoeuvre brought him closer, and soon he would be so near that the ground fire could not touch him for fear of hitting the balloon.

"That Archie-fire isn't so hot," Bill observed, glancing up from his notes. "It won't stop that bird. Gosh! He's a pretty flyer."

"Yeah! Three cheers for the handsome undertaker."

"No, Sir! That ground fire is too full o' holes. He's going to adjourn our party in a few minutes. Here he comes. Boy, let's go!"

Bill hitched himself into a contraption suspended from above the basket. The other man did likewise and then gathered Rags into his arms. Bill shouted, "All overboard!" and a second later Rags found himself falling into space. The abrupt descent was checked suddenly as the parachute filled. Rags and his companion were floating toward the earth.

Rags wriggled restlessly as his ears caught the familiar "ker-ping" of passing bullets, and he saw the Fokker like a great roaring bird, diving at him. Rags wasn't afraid of birds, no matter how much noise they made. He twisted and tried to bark at it, but he was being held too closely to get much defiance into his voice.

"That bird isn't scared of terriers, doggie," the observer told Rags, "so there's no use of barking at him. Take it easy or you'll make me drop you!"

Then, of a sudden, the enemy pilot poked his helmeted, goggled head over the cockpit, hesitated a minute, grinned, and waved his hand. The plane banked sharply, and, twisting, zooming, and dodging, to avoid the ground fire, soared away toward the enemy lines. Rags shifted again in an attempt to bark after it.

"Don't get sore at that balloon-buster, puppy," the observer advised. "He was a pretty good sport. He was out to get me, so I wouldn't be spillin' any secrets from his side o' the fence, and he'd have made it if he hadn't passed up the job on account o' you."

The parachute settled in a field about a mile from the balloon station. Hardly had the observer's feet touched the ground than Rags was snatched from his arms. Donovan, who had been following the descent of the parachute, stringing wire as he went, thrust field telephone into the man's hand.

"Division G-2 is on there," he growled, "and they want your final report."

When the conversation was finished the observer called to Rags, but the terrier paid no attention to him and followed Donovan as the sergeant supervised the taking up of the wire.

"Listen, mister," the sergeant informed Rags, "You'd better hot-foot it back to the artillery and stick around there for a while. I don't want any more fool balloonists risking your neck, and where I'm going isn't any place for you. Go on. Be sensible. Beat it!"

Rags liked Donovan's speeches to him. Also he had a pretty idea of the sergeant's meaning. Instead of obeying, he sat down in front of Donovan, thumped his tail emphatically, and barked.

"Well," Donovan continued, judicially, "if you feel that way about it, it's your funeral. But here's the lay-out. The boss wants to turn any guns captured from the enemy against them. Our job is to trail along with the front-line infantry and string a wire from any gun we happen to collect, so the doughboys can tell the redlegs where to shoot it and when. Soissons was a nice quiet party compared with what this is goin' to be. What's the sense of letting yourself in for a lot of bad luck."

Rags placed his forepaws against Donovan's knees and gazed up at him, panting pleadingly.

"Come on," said the sergeant, "but don't say I didn't tip you off."

Rags gave a satisfied bark and kept close to Donovan's heels as the sergeant made his preparations for moving. The dog sulked a bit as Donovan fitted and tested a new gas mask for him. It was a less clumsy arrangement than the one he formerly had been forced to wear, so he submitted to the adjusting. But he balked at carrying it around his neck. As fast as Donovan tied the bag containing the mask on Rags, the terrier pawed, wriggled, and squirmed until he got rid of it. Donovan gave up.

"You'd better stick close to me, then," he told Rags, "for if you don't lug this an' we get gas, you won't even look natural."

Rags kept close to Donovan when the sergeant went to headquarters for final instructions, and edged himself into a place at the sergeant's feet when they boarded the truck that was carrying the signalmen to the jumping-off stations. When the doughboys moved, Rags nearly tripped a lieutenant as he ran through the officer's legs to take up his post next to Donovan. The sergeant's job wasn't fighting, but he was a seasoned soldier, and when a squad leader fell he took command, distributing his individual cargo of telephone material among the other soldiers, who welcomed his leadership. Thus, with Rags at his side, he moved forward,

27

crawling, running, wriggling along the ground keeping his little group neck and neck with the other doughboys.

The cannon din was deafening. There was a regiment of American artillery supporting each infantry regiment and a record-breaking massing of heavy guns in the rear—a combined concentration of fire that was smothering the enemy guns. The barrage rolled ahead of the infantry, churning up the ground, tearing up the wire, leveling the trench parapets, but missing a great many machine-gun nests. These, from the most unexpected angles, poured a raking fire into the advancing doughboys. Rags took his cues from Donovan and wriggled along the ground or dashed forward in imitation of the sergeant's movements.

Donovan crawled through a gap in some tangled barbed wire. Rags squirmed along beside him, catching his fuzzy coat in some of the sharp barbs, but tearing loose in the excitement of the advance and leaving little tufts of olive-drab hair marking his course through entanglements. Tumbling into a trench behind Donovan, Rags got his first view of hand-to-hand fighting. Big men in grey uniforms fell upon Donovan's attacking party, stabbing, clubbing, and shooting. Rags tried to nip one of them who was pressing Donovan hard. His teeth slipped off the tough greased boot which protected the man's lower leg. He tried again, but, still unable to make any impression, shifted his attack to above the knee. The man tried to shake him off. It was too late. The dog had supplied the diversion Donovan needed. The trench was taken. The American advance swept on.

As the drive bit deeper into the hostile line it became apparent to Donovan that the enemy had removed most of his cannon and material before falling back. But suddenly an abandoned howitzer loomed ahead. With a whoop of delight Donovan dashed for it, followed by his command, now augmented by remnants of other squads. A burst of machine-gun fire from a nest in front of the gun cooled his ardor. He signaled his men to take cover and deploy. With a picked detail he made a detour and took the nest in the rear. The defenders met the attack without flinching. A gray-clad giant closed with Donovan, and the sergeant, caught off balance, stumbled and fell, with the enemy on top, clutching the American's throat with one hand and trying to swing a clubbed Mauser pistol with the other. Rags leaped for the hand that held the pistol. As his teeth sank into the man's wrist the pistol clattered to the ground. The grip on Donovan's throat relaxed. The sergeant shook the man from him, and after a few minutes of desperate fighting the Americans mopped up the nest.

Donovan gave his attention to the captured howitzer. There was little ammunition, but enough to harass a retiring enemy for a few moments. With the help of all the men he could muster, he swung the gun around toward the retreating foe.

He had been informed, when the attack began, that artillerymen trained in the operation of enemy ordnance would be attached to the infantry, and began casting around for one of these—neither he nor any of the men with him knew anything about the mechanism of the big howitzer—but the search was futile. There was not an artilleryman in sight.

"Now that we've got this thing," he confided to his men, "I'd like to do something with it. But I don't savvy any of these gadgets on it, an' all of you guys are just as dumb."

The soldiers nodded their heads in sad agreement. They too wanted to see the captured piece in operation.

Donovan gazed meditatively at Rags.

"Say, old-timer," he addressed the little terrier, "I'll bet if I started you back toward the batteries you'd dig out a stray redleg that would know how to make this thing perform!"

Rags, still panting a bit and aquiver with excitement, stiffened and barked toward the enemy lines.

"Face the other way, as Mr. Sheridan said," Donovan chuckled, "I'll bet a month's pay you can do it."

The sergeant scrawled a note. It was addressed "to any officer," gave the location of the captured gun, and requested that an artillerist be sent to show the doughboys how to put the piece into action. He folded it neatly and started Rags toward the batteries. The dog had forgotten none of his previous training and set off at a lope.

"He'll dig out somebody," Donovan assured his followers.

Rags did. In a few minutes he came trotting back with the platoon commander.

"Never mind that piece of junk," the officer told Donovan. "We don't need it. Ditch that signal-corps stuff you're packing and keep on with us. We've got more artillery support now than we need. It's slowing us up."

"You mean I should act as infantry, sir?" Donovan inquired.

"That's what you've been doing, isn't it? And you've been doing fine. Keep at it. Forget the signal business for a while. Glad I met up with that dog o' yours."

"What'll we do with this gun, sir?" Donovan wanted to know.

29

"Keep it for a watch charm, or make the dog a collar out of it. Who cares? Get goin' as soon as can. We're ten minutes ahead o' schedule now, there's no tellin' when we'll hit a block. And the Boy is sure hell on schedules."

The officer hurried away. Shells were falling now and then, but there was a lull in the intensive small-arms fire that had hampered the advance in its earlier hours. Donovan realized that the enemy was retreating and that with the taking of the nest at the howitzer he probably had squelched the last advanced defense in his immediate sector.

"We might as well get a breath and a bite," he told his little force. "We probably won't hit another hot spot for upward of half a mile. Anyhow, Rags here, and me, need a rest, an' I don't hear any o' you gents yellin' for settin'-up exercises."

In the shelter of the nest Donovan shared his "iron rations" with Rags, and gave the dog some water out of his canteen. The little terrier was panting from his exertions, and, having finished his meal, curled up for a nap. In about ten minutes Donovan glanced at his wristwatch. The mud-caked men around him had followed the example of Rags. All were catching a nap. He roused them and noticed that one, Private Cohen, had a bandaged wrist, a limp, and other symptoms of having stopped hostile missiles.

"Say, Ikey," Donovan addressed Cohen, "you've been hit a couple of times. Beat it back. You'll get a medal, maybe, and a nice rest. An' take Rags with you. He's done his share an' I don't want him hurt."

Cohen demurred, but Donovan insisted. He admired Cohen's pluck—but he wanted to get Rags in a safe place.

"Take the dog with you, Ike, and turn him over to Artillery P. C."

Ike gathered the sleeping Rags under his arm and started limping rearward. Rags awakened. There was a flurry of fur, a string of protests from Cohen, and Rags came trotting back into the nest. Ikey arrived a few minutes later. He faced Donovan with an expressive shrug.

"Vell?"

"Vell what?" snapped Donovan. "Why don't you take the dog an' beat it out o' here?"

"Oi! Vy don't I? Vy don't you esk de dog?"

Rags stood growling menacingly at Cohen. It was plain the terrier didn't intend to be separated from Donovan.

"Okay, Ikey," the sergeant laughed. "I get your point. But you might as well beat it. We're shovin' in a minute or two."

"I should beat it? For vy, I esk you? De dog von't go, so vy should

30

Ikey Cohen? Em I a cripple dot I should go vay ven a Jew is mit de vinners, en' let Irishers en Scotchers get all de medals, mebbe?"

Donovan grinned. "It's your funeral, Ikey. If you want to stick along it's okay with me."

"Oi, en' spikin" ov funerals, Meester Donovan, vud it be good beezness, I esk you, for a seek men like me to go home mebbe an' buy 'is own funeral, ven he should get vun here for noddings?"

That sally, which Cohen made with a grin, brought a roaring laugh that was also a cheer as the outfit shoved off again.

CHAPTER SIX
THE MESSAGE-BEARER

A weary, mud-caked, group of infantrymen slogged through the mud on the La Marche-Nonsar road. Artillery, rumbling along beside them, churned the shell-torn highway and spattered the yellow-green muck over their uniforms. The First Division was being relieved. In four days of fighting it had expended its last ounce of energy. Some of the men appeared to be asleep as they marched. Their feet moved automatically, without any consciousness on the part of the soldiers. Rags staggered along sleepily beside Donovan, who dozed as he marched.

As the doughboys came abreast of the Seventh Field Artillery, which was moving out of La Marche, Donovan lifted the tired little terrier to the top of an ammunition-box, and started ahead to report to the artillery commander and rejoin the signal detail.

Rags dropped into a doze the moment he landed on the box, but as Donovan moved away he sat up, wide awake, jumped off the caisson, and followed the sergeant. He gave a tired, low bark to attract Donovan's attention.

"None o' that, now," the sergeant told him. "I'm not going anywhere, and you're all tired out. Get back on that box!"

Rags wagged his tail and gazed pleadingly at Donovan. The sergeant picked him up and set him atop a shell compartment.

"Now, stay there," he ordered. "I'll be back after a while and you might as well ride."

He started off again. So did Rags.

"The pup won't let you shake him," sang out a comaneer.

"I don't want to shake him," Donovan replied, "but I've got to find the skipper and report. I've been A. W. O. L. with infantry for four days. But the dog's all in. He's got to ride."

"Why don't you ride with him? We're going into rest in the Bois de la Belle Oziere. You can catch the Old Man there. There's a truck train back a ways on the road, with some signal stuff. Why don't you hop it with the pooch and travel right?"

Donovan thanked the man and sat down by the side of the road to wait for the trucks. Rags curled up in the mud and went to sleep, with his nose resting against the sergeant's feet.

The trucks came chugging up. The driver of the first one hailed Donovan.

"Climb on, you big loafer," he invited. "We'd figured you an' Rags had gone west, until we heard you were medal-snatching with the foot soldiers."

"We've got an alibi," Donovan remonstrated as he lifted Rags to the truck and climbed aboard. "We were ordered to be infantry, so infantry we were."

"Yeah, so we've been hearing. The skipper has been sayin' a few words about it. He ain't blamin' you, after what he's been tellin' the infantry, no ninety-day wonder is makin' cannon fodder out o' high-priced signalmen pretty soon again, you bet you."

"Was he sore?"

"Boy, if you could o' seen him an' heard him, you'd o' guessed he wasn't only sore, he was racked with pain. He sure knows a lot o' words."

"Guess I must be sittin' pretty with the Old Man if he was worried like that about me."

"He wasn't worryin' about you. But he figures when you grab a harp Rags'll stick around with him. An' he don't want nothin' to happen to Rags."

"Aw, go dive in the gold-fish bowl."

The truck-driver chuckled with satisfaction ."Got your goat, didn't I?" he observed.

But Donovan, after days of trying to sleep on his feet, was draped over the piles of wire and other material, dead to the world. Rags moved in his sleep until his nose was against the sergeant's outflung hand. The driver surveyed them and muttered to himself:

"Clean out, both of 'em. Could sleep on a pile of broken bottles.

Donovan and Rags were still sleeping when the truck pulled into Bois de la Belle Oziere. Rags awakened at the driver's shout, Donovan slumbered on until shaken forcefully.

"Change cars," the truckman announced. "End o' the line. They got the 'flu' here an' the division is being shoved on to Bois d'Ahaye."

Donovan detrained wearily from the truck and, with Rags following, reported to his captain. Then he hunted up another lorry and slept his way into the Bois d'Ahaye rest area.

In Bois d'Ahaye Donovan and Rags acquired quarters and were just about getting caught up with their sleep when, on the morning of September 27, 1918, word was passed along the line that the division was to move. Donovan, again back with the signalmen, accompanied the Seventh Field Artillery.

By forced marches the division traveled as a relief unit to the

Meuse-Argonne. The Seventh Field took up a position back of the Very-Epinonville road, south-west of Eclisfontaine. Communications were perfect, and when the cannoneers moved into position it looked as if Donovan—and Rags—would have little to do except load around the regimental command post. But the artillerymen had hardly dropped their trails when messages began coming through. Infantry was driving forward and it wanted support. The enemy defense was stiffening. Would the redlegs please get busy? The redlegs did.

Not all the guns were placed when the seventy-fives of the Seventh began tossing shell. Then, as the doughboys pushed forward, communications began breaking down. Hostile cannon were throwing a demolition barrage between the infantry and its artillery support. The gunners, after a time, found themselves out of touch with the infantry, and the guns became silent. Cannon cannot fire when there is a chance that shell may hit their own troops. Donovan and his trouble-shooting signalmen crawled forward to hunt up the breaks in the wire. Rags wriggled along beside the sergeant. The enemy barrage was intense. It made the terrain a sea of spouting, unstable ground.

In the early hours of the movement, Rags expedited Donovan's work by racing along the wire and stopping to bark when he came to a break. Then the enemy began throwing gas. With his nose put out of action and his vision blurred by his mask, Rags was unable to do more than keep beside Donovan and lend his moral support to the adventure. Together they reached the body of a runner—his field message clutched in his hand. Donovan ripped it open and read it. His eyes bogged! With renewed energy he flung himself at the wire. A dozen futile attempts to find a line that had not been cut behind him and he groaned in despair. A furry body nudged him and Donovan yelped. Rags! Rags would carry on!

He tied the message to the gas mask and urged the dog rearward, toward the artillery post of command. At first Rags did not understand. He had always carried messages in his mouth. But under Donovan's urging and coaxing he started. In less than a quarter of an hour he was back. The artillery was hurling shell into a wood that had been holding up the infantry. How Rags relayed that message is one of the mysteries of the Meuse-Argonne campaign. Rags himself can't tell. And no record of the identity of the person who got it to its destination appears. But the message itself is on file. It read:

From C.O. 1st Btn. 26th Infantry:
Oct 2 - 12.30 p.m.:

To Captain Thomas, Intelligence Officer:
Have artillery that is firing in small, oblong-shaped woods, directly in front and on right of first objective, lengthen range and pound hell out of the woods. Machine-gun nests are located there.
Legge, cdg.

Donovan was struggling with his wires when some guns of the Seventh Field, acting on information brought through by airplane observers, "leap-frogged" him and pushed up close behind the infantry, north and slightly west, of Eclisfontaine. Exhausted, he crawled into a shell hole with Rags and slept.

The morning of the 3rd dawned crisp and clear. The advance had driven forward and there was no gas. Donovan removed the gas mask—in which he had slept—and also relieved Rags of the contraption, which nearly had smothered the tired terrier as he had tried to sleep.

The sergeant poked his head over the top of the shell hole and noticed a doughboy detail moving rearward, guarding prisoners.

Heading the procession was a corporal and an enemy major who was protesting loudly—in precise Oxford English—against the humiliation of being compelled to march with private soldiers. The corporal was not taking the protests very seriously. Donovan grinned. But Rags gave a low growl and advanced belligerently on the major. The terrier had not forgotten those gray-clad warriors of the St.-Mihiel. Crouching low—as if waiting for Donovan to take the initiative—the dog advanced on the officer, growling menacingly. The prisoner kicked viciously at him, landing a heavy boot squarely on the terrier's mid-ribs. Rags made no sound. He rolled over, caught his breath, and gathered himself for a leap. The corporal, with a sudden realization that it was his duty to guard his prisoner, lowered his rifle and stepped in front of the captured major.

Donovan clambered out of the shell hole and gathered Rags into his arms. He turned to one of the soldiers of the convoy.

"Hold that dog," he snapped, "and don't hurt him."

Then he advanced to the major.

"Mister," he growled, "I'm going to give you the trimmim' of your life. That's a soldier dog, an' no brass-hatted kraut-eater is kickin' him around an' getting away with it."

The major came to a stiff attention. There was contempt in his voice; his words clipped bitingly.

"To beat a prisoner would be an heroic adventure for a Yankee!" he rasped.

35

The corporal shouldered in between Donovan and the prisoner, pushing the sergeant back with a sudden thrust of his rifle, then swinging the bayonet to the front.

"Listen, big boy," he announced, "I'll do all the trimmin' around here. When this bird needs anything he can get it from me. I don't crave no outside assistance at all."

"Listen yourself!" Donovan shot back. "That dog o' mine was through St.-Mihiel with me. An' yesterday he carried a message that saved some o' you guys from bein' angels. I'm aimin' to trim this bird on the square if he ain't afraid to fight. Let us battle it out with dukes an' if he licks me turn him loose."

"Nothin' doin' on the turnin'-loose stuff," the corporal ruled. "But if he wants to take you on, that's okay with us. If he mops up a sergeant, maybe we'll donate a carton o' cigarettes an' some vin rouge to him."

He turned to the captured enemy.

"You spretchen English. How about it?"

"I shall be most happy to oblige the sergeant, but I desire to apologize to the little dog. He is a brave little fellow and he would not hate us if he knew us."

The man clicked his heels and faced the soldier who held Rags. He saluted as snappily as if he were in the presence of his high commander. A stray long-range shell came groaning through the air. It dropped a few hundred feet from the group, but some of the mud it churned up spattered them.

"Guess you birds better do your Jeffries-Johnson in the shell hole," the corporal commented.

The officer turned to him.

"May I remove my tunic?" he inquired.

"Sure, mister. From what I know about these hard-boiled sergeants, you won't want to be packing any excess weight. An' we're all pullin' for you to trim the sarge."

"Perhaps it would be only fair to warn the sergeant that I am a skilled boxer," the major observed.

Donovan already shedding his belt, pack, and blouse, merely grunted:

"Get goin'. Don't hold up the parade. And leave your name and address with the room clerk."

The major slipped off his uniform coat, tossed his shirt after it, and stood flexing his rippling muscles while Donovan growled orders at the soldier who held Rags.

"Back up," he snapped. "You couldn't hold the dog if I was getting the worst of it! Keep him where he can't see it."

Shouting to the prisoner to follow, the sergeant slid down to the bottom of the shell hole. The uneven surface was made to order for Donovan's style of fighting—rush in, get set, take the other fellow's wallops, and outslug him. Donovan's first rush was checked by a straight left, followed by a vicious right hook. But the major was standing on a couple of unstable slabs of earth and much of the steam was out of the blows when they landed. Donovan recovered and rushed, driving hard jabs to the German's midriff. The major stumbled, recovered his balance, and took a stiff body hammering without flinching in an effort to set himself. Finding a solid piece of mud, he blocked, side-slipped until Donovan gave him an opening. Then he drove a stinging one-two for the jaw. Donovan slipped on a rolling shell fragment and staggered backward, the punches missing him by inches. The major attempted to follow his advantage, and, stepping out of his solid bank of mud, stumbled and was falling forward as Donovan recovered. The sergeant's fist caught him squarely on the point of the jaw—the "button." He dropped and the soldiers at the top of the hole began counting raucously, "One-two-three-four-five-six-seven ——"

The officer began to struggle to his feet, Donovan stepping back to give him time to recover. When he had gained his feet Donovan rushed again. The officer went into a clinch, hanging on for grim life and smothering Donovan's blows, to gain time until his head had cleared from the stupefying smash the American had landed. Half a head shorter than Donovan, and slimmer than the husky sergeant, he was, to the signalman's surprise, his match in strength, more than his match in wrestling skill.

With a sudden twist and quick push he drove the sergeant halfway across the shell hole, and retreated to a hard slab of earth on which he could move a few feet in either direction and fend off Donovan's attack with his swift, cutting jabs. Donovan, recognizing that his opponent held the advantage, and realizing from the blows that had landed that he was a terrific hitter, began circling for a rush. He backed away a few feet, charged, and, as he came within range of that stinging left, shifted to one side and tried for a solar-plexus punch. He tripped and fell sprawling. The enemy officer, returning Donovan's courtesy, and backing away until the sergeant could get up, caught his spur in a chunk of clay and fell backward. Then came an interruption. As Donovan staggered to his feet a furry ball of fury rolled down the side of the shell hole and dived for

37

the officer's throat. The soldier who had been charged with holding Rags, had been drawn to the edge of the shell hole by the interest of his comrades, and the dog, in a sudden wrench, had wrested himself free and rushed to the aid of Donovan. The sergeant caught him barely in time to save the officer, who got to his feet as Donovan was retreating with Rags in his arms. The man came to a stiff attention and saluted.

"I thank you," he said. "You are a sportsman."

"Yeah," said Donovan. "You ain't so bad yourself. If it's okay with you we'll adjourn this session. I can't trust those dumbbells on top to keep Rags out of it, and what I started out to do was to hand you a trimmin', not to get you assassinated. We'll go up top and put those other birds down here."

The corporal vetoed that plan.

"I've got to deliver these prisoners," he explained, "an" I've wasted a lot o' time as it is. Fall in, Mister Major! On your way, Sergeant!"

As the convoy moved on, one of the prisoners flung a piece of sausage to Rags. The terrier, who had been living on short rations since arriving in the battle zone, fell on it greedily. Donovan rushed for Rags.

"Hey, you!" he shouted, "Drop it! Maybe it's poisoned."

By the time he reached the terrier and snatched the food from him, Rags had eaten about half of it. Donovan shook his fist after the retreating convoy,

"If there's poison in that," he shouted, "I'll take it out on all of your relations, an' don't forget it!"

CHAPTER SEVEN
SEEING IT THROUGH

RAGS gazed longingly at the piece of sausage Donovan had snatched from him. He sat up, telling, as plainly as a dog could, that, if his friend needed the food, it was all right. If Donovan wasn't going to eat it, Rags could use it. Worried, Donovan ignored the pleading, and gazed doubtfully after the retreating convoy. Rags coughed; then sneezed, intensifying the sergeant's fear that the food had been poisoned. Donovan ran after the prisoners until he caught up with the corporal in charge of them.

"What's bitin' you now?" the corporal asked.

"I'm afraid that guy poisoned my dog!"

"How come?"

"Didn't you see him throw a sausage to Rags, just as you shoved off?"

"Nope. But why should he want to poison the pup?"

"Why should he want to feed him?"

"Search me. But let's find out if he did. The pooch looks all right to me."

"How'll we find out?"

"Make the guy eat what's left o' the sausage. If he balks, maybe it's doped. If he don't, it's prob'ly okay. Hey, Schwartz!"

One of the guards hurried up.

"Try your Milwaukee German on that guy," the corporal ordered, indicating the prisoner who had offered the sausage to Rags. "Ask him what he thinks he's doin' tryin' to poison a Yank dog. Tell him if the grub was on the level he's got to prove it by eatin' it."

Schwartz spoke sharply to the captive. The man lifted his hands in a gesture of protest, reached for the sausage and gulped it down. Then he spoke at length in low tones, to Schwartz, while the other prisoners clustered around and nodded. One of them fished another sausage from his pocket, ate a piece of it, and offered it to Donovan for the dog. Satisfied, the sergeant passed it to Rags, who barked his thanks and fell to. Schwartz and the prisoner kept on talking.

"What's all the private confab about?" the corporal growled.

Schwartz grinned, and started to answer just as Donovan cut in.

"Why are these guys so anxious to slip Rags a handout?" the sergeant demanded.

"I'm comin' to that," Schwartz informed him. "It seems this major we collected was one hard-boiled hombre with the buck privates—one o' these big-hearted guys that would give a soldier a lot of extra duty for sneezin' in ranks. Our little playmates were so tickled to see Rags an' the sergeant muss up his dignity that they wanted to show their appreciation."

He doesn't seem like such a bad guy," Donovan commentated.

"No worse an' no better than the rest of them. They spell discipline in capital letters an' write it in red in that man's army. My old man was in it 'fore he went to America, an' I've heard him tell plenty."

"Well, tell 'em much obliged. Guess Rags an' me'll be goin'."

The convoy moved off. Donovan and the terrier headed in the opposite direction, the sergeant admonishing the dog as they walked.

"Don't be so fast grabbin' handouts from strangers," he advised. "It was all right that time, but, old-timer, you gave me a bunch o' gray hairs until I found out it was on the level. Gettin' poisoned is no way for a soldier to check out."

The "big push" had left Donovan and Rags behind. They caught up, somewhere around Serieux Ferme, pushed ahead, and made contact with the Seventh Field Artillery. Donovan resumed his job of keeping communications with the infantry open—a job that grew more difficult as the advance progressed. When there was freedom from gas, Rags aided by following the lines with his nose until he found a break. Then he would halt and bark. When he was handicapped by his gas mask the terrier merely followed Donovan. The nerve-tearing racket of the artillery didn't bother him. But he never failed to sense the approach of a shell. The intensity of the fighting increased. The Twenty-sixth Infantry was driving through the valley between Hills 272 and 269, after the Ferme d'Arietal had fallen. The doughboys were advancing with their "flanks refused"—a modernistic military adaptation of the famous British square—heading toward the gloomy catacombs of Le Petit Bois.

Donovan had finished patching his lines when a heavy box barrage dropped, and a stiff counter-attack was launched on the right of the Americans. The infantry commander tried to get the artillery on his telephone. The line was broken. A runner was started rearward; he had only about four hundred yards to go, so closely were the cannoneers supportin' the doughboys. The barrage cut him down. Rags found him and led Donovan to him. The sergeant took the message, tested his lines until he got through to artillery, and read it to them.

Soon the seventy-fives of the Seventh were crashing their shells into the wood. The counter-attack was checked. But the box barrage with which the enemy had tried to support its counter-smash had torn the telephone lines to shreds. The fire continued long after the thrust was stopped. To attempt to patch wire under a cannonade was suicidal. Donovan and Rags crept into a shell hole and slept. The terrier's hunger was their alarm clock. It was dark when the dog nosed Donovan into wakefulness. The sergeant shared his rations with Rags, hunted up the artillery positions, and made his preparations for the next day's activity.

A thick fog hung over the Argonne on the morning of October 9, 1918. Ordinarily it would have paralyzed military activities. But the American high command was smashing through for a decision. It did not purpose to be robbed of the fruits of days of grueling fighting—the drive started on September 26th—by any mist, no matter how heavy. The enemy was backing up, contesting every inch of ground. The Americans wanted to keep him backing up. Any relaxation of the attack would give him a chance to dig in and halt the big parade. So, ignoring the fog, the Yanks pressed ahead.

Donovan and hundreds of other signalmen who were scattered through the zone, keeping the guns in touch with the foot soldiers, could see only a few feet through the fog. Seeking wire was like diving for pennies in a big tank of milk. The mist blanket blunted the sergeant's hearing. He could not catch the approach of shell as quickly as usual. He took his cues from Rags, whose hearing seemed unimpaired and who flattened himself before the sergeant even suspected a projectile was on its way. The fire grew more vicious as the day wore on. The American batteries were pounding the advanced lines of the enemy as lines never had been hammered before. The advanced, lighter pieces of hostile cannon were forced out of action. With heavy guns located far in the rear the foe began searching the terrain for the Yank seventy-fives. The big shells landed with volcanic upheavals of ground, playing havoc with the wires. Donovan and Rags groped through the mist. Rags's keen nose found the wire Donovan could not see. The dog led along it until the gap was found. But even with Rags's help, the job was nearly hopeless. Almost as fast as Donovan got the line working in one place it went out of commission somewhere else. Sometimes the break was in his own section. Again it was in the sections in front of or behind him.

Each hour of fighting made the line more vulnerable. The doughboys pushed ahead through Le Petit Bois. The artillery post of command remained near La Neuville le Comte Ferme, about two kilometers in the rear. Communications lines grew longer and longer.

Strain on the signalmen at the extreme front was somewhat relieved by special details sent out by the First Engineers, who were now fighting on the right of the Twenty-sixth Infantry. The artillery end of the lines continued to suffer from demolition fire. Donovan mended a break; on test he found his line working. There was a sudden slackening of fire, both by the Americans and by the enemy. The sergeant slipped into a shell hole; Rags curled up at his feet and dropped into a doze. Donovan did not dare close his eyes. He stretched flat on his back and relaxed. For a few moments there was a silence so deep that Donovan's heartbeats set up a roaring in his ears. Rags stretched and whimpered in his sleep. A big shell band with a loose band rattled overhead like a train with flat wheels. It dropped far to the right—a dud. The fog, which had been slowly thinning, lifted and drifted away. The sky was a sickly gray. It reminded Donovan of the peculiar heaviness before a cyclone in his native Middle West.

The storm broke with a crash. Without any preliminary ranging shots, the enemy seemed to concentrate every gun on this little patch of ground. The curtain of fire fell about two hundred meters back of Donovan. He was safe enough in his shell hole unless the enemy shortened the range. Realizing that an interdiction barrage was falling, and wondering why his own artillery was silent, Donovan cut in on the line beside which he was resting. He picked up a message from an officer who had been trying to raise the artillery. The infantry had taken Hill 263. They were digging in. An enemy counter-attack was massing. Artillery fire was needed. Unless it was forthcoming promptly the men on the hill would be driven out by sheer force of numbers. With the American cannon silent, the enemy was free to fling heavy reserves at the hill. Donovan carefully wrote out the positions of the assaulting forces and a brief explanation of the situation. He promised to try to get the message through.

Meantime, the curtain of fire behind him spread, fanwise, and rolled toward the rear. With Rags, he clambered from the shell hole and ran along the wire. He found it reduced to scrap for a good fifty wards where the barrage first had fallen. A choking sensation gripped him. He clapped on his gas mask. Rags sneezed and pawed his nose. Closer to the ground than Donovan, the dog got a stronger whiff of the poison. Donovan, gasping himself, picked him up, adjusted his mask and hurried along the wire, searching for the other end of the break. He found it and cut in with his field set, only to discover it was open farther on. He was on the edge of the barrage now. Before he reached a new break he was in the thick of it. Glancing at his wristwatch, he decided it was high time the guns got busy if they were to do any good. His patrol along the wire had brought him to within a kilometer of the Second Battalion of the Seventh artillery which was hidden on the southeast slope of Hill 212.

After a futile effort to telephone the message, Donovan decided to waste no more time on the wires. He would carry the message through. He realized that one purpose of the enemy fire curtain had been to tear communications to pieces.

Quickly memorizing the positions, Donovan tied the note he had made from the infantry message to Rags's collar and started the dog toward the guns. A terrific blast sent both of them sprawling. Metal showered about them. A shell splinter cut Rags's left forepaw. Another caromed off his gas mask, mangling his right ear. A needle-like sliver was imbedded under his right eye. The terrier was dazed for a minute. Then he struggled to his feet. Donovan lay where he had fallen. His gas mask had been shot away; arms and legs were cut by shrapnel. Blood from a gash in his forehead was blinding him. Over all hung the burning tang of gas—thinned somewhat by a northwest breeze, but still strong enough to sear the throats of sergeant and terrier. Between wheezes and coughs Rags pawed the now useless mask from his head. He licked first the sergeant's outflung hand, then his face. Donovan roused himself. He lengthened the wire that tied the message to the dog's collar, so Rags could carry the paper in his mouth. It would be lost if the little terrier succumbed before delivering it. The sergeant started the dog toward the guns. As nearby bursts intensified the gas, Donovan staggered to his feet and urged the dog to a run. The terrier, favoring his wounded paw as much as he could, moved at a limping trot. Donovan, stumbling along behind, saw the concussion of a nearby shell-blast turn the little terrier on his back.

Rags was rolled over the edge of a shell hole by the force of the explosion. He fell almost into the arms of a liaison man, sent out from the artillery end to repair the broken line. The soldier noticed the message, still tightly clamped in the terrier's teeth. He read it, and cut in on the wire end he had dragged into the shell hole. But there was no answer. The fire had cut the line behind him. Tucking the still gasping Rags under his arm, the man raced rearward to the foot of Hill 212, taking time to pick holes in the fire curtain. Shifting drum fire was beating the face of the hill. The soldier circled around the base. He reached the battalion command post just ahead of a couple of observers, who were half carrying a sergeant they had picked up on the brow of the hill.

An officer—frantic because he could not give the infantry support until he knew where they were—read the message and began barking orders. His adjutant grabbed a telephone and passed them on to the guns. Rags lay on the floor of the dugout, pawing wistfully at the wire that still was fastened to his collar. The battalion commander stooped and removed it. As he tossed it aside the observers brought in the man they had found on the brow of the hill.

It was Donovan. The sergeant, although badly wounded, had come up the face of the elevation through the barrage. He had been hit again as he neared the crest. The observers had dragged him to shelter. He had mumbled something about a message —had asked whether a dog got through. The officer recognized Donovan.

"It's all right, Sergeant," he said. "We got your message. Everything's okay!"

As he spoke the first salvo from the guns jarred the dugout.

"There they go," mumbled Donovan. "Good 'ol Rags. He made it."

From the sergeant's disjointed sentences the men pieced together the story of what had happened after Rags was started with the message. Donovan had seen the dog rolled over by the shell-blast and had himself been knocked down by another. When he regained his senses, Rags was nowhere in sight. The sergeant decided the little terrier had been killed and struggled through the fire himself to bring the message.

Donovan crumpled in the arms of the observers. They lowered him gently to the floor. The commander called his orderly.

"Get some men and take the sergeant and this dog to a dressing-station. Tell them the dog is to get the same treatment as a soldier. Both are to go back to a hospital in the first available transportation."

Rags crept to the side of Donovan, stuck his nose against the sergeant's head, and dropped into a coma. Both were lifted to the same stretcher and carried to the dressing-station. A young medical officer gave them first aid, tagged them "serious," and started them toward a base-hospital train.

CHAPTER EIGHT
WOUNDED VETERANS

THE ambulance men, when they reached the dressing-station, were reluctant to transport a dog. One of them started to lift Rags from the foot of Donovan's stretcher. A wounded artilleryman, awaiting his turn for a leg dressing, limped across the dugout.

"What you doin'" to that dog?" he demanded.

"Ditchin' him," the ambulance man explained. "Got all we can without haulin' any dogs."

The wounded cannoneer balanced himself on his good leg and clenched his fists. Briefly and forcefully he told about Rags's trip through the barrage. The ambulance men were appreciative. They agreed that the dog rated attention, but it was against the regulations. The artilleryman was insistent. There was an order giving Rags all the privileges of a soldier, he declared.

"Get us an order from an officer," one of the ambulance men told him, "and we'll see the little pup through."

"Now you're talkin'," the cannoneer grinned. "I'll get it, toot sweet."

The medical officer was curt. Almost asleep on his feet, he was working more by instinct than by any conscious activity. For more than twenty-four hours he had been caring for the wounded who found their way, or were carried, to his station. He remembered through his haze of fatigue, that there was a dog hero among his patients, and that a special order covered him.

"Take the pup," he snapped. "Orders from headquarters."

That was enough for the ambulance men. They loaded Donovan and Rags into their vehicle with other casuals, and began the risky trip to the division field hospital. There was a big red cross painted on the roof of the ambulance. Whether the enemy flyers didn't know what it meant, or whether it was too good a target to resist, nobody ever will know. Every now and then some aviator dived and emptied a machine belt at it. The drivers moved at the swiftest pace their motors would give, hurdling the shell holes they couldn't dodge. Donovan and Rags were on the top "shelf" of that ambulance. An airplane bullet plugged through the roof, tore between Donovan's feet and Rags, and killed the soldier on the bottom stretcher. The mud-guards of the ambulance were riddled. Two tires were hit. The ambulance limped to its destination on a pair of flats.

At the field hospital, overworked doctors and nurses protested against being asked to treat a dog. The ambulance crew passed on their instructions; "Orders from headquarters!"

To the division medical staff "headquarters" meant the division commander—General Summerall. Everybody knew that the same person never fumbled the general's orders more than once. There never was a second chance. Blunderers were transferred to places where, if they bungled things, the mix-up did not affect the general's plans. So, in the big tent where Donovan's bandages were inspected and changed, Rags's wounds also were redressed. A weary nurse, her sympathies aroused by the terrier's unwhimpering stoicism, used the few minutes she had been allowed for a nap to force broth from a spoon down the dog's throat.

Bound for base hospital, Donovan and Rags once more were loaded into an ambulance and the journey rearward was resumed. The ambulance halted at an intermediate dressing-station—dressings were inspected, but changed only if the need was urgent. Doctors expressed surprise that a dog was traveling in an ambulance. The ambulance crew repeated the phrase that had become Rags's password:

"Orders from headquarters," they explained. "The dog gets attention same as a soldier."

The medicos were proud of their division chief, and if he wanted a dog attended to they were glad to oblige. Most of the wounded merely got inspection. Donovan and Rags were given new dressings. Then with ponchos to keep them dry, they were sent out in the rain to await the ambulance that would take them to the evacuation hospital.

Again came the question of carrying the dog. Once more the old formula was invoked, "Orders from headquarters!"

For the fourth time it worked.

At the evacuation hospital a young medical officer made a swift survey of Donovan's injuries and ordered him to the operating-room. This was a big tent with about two dozen operating-tables ranged in rows. It had a vestibule in which the wounded awaited their turns. Here the diagnosis was made.

A doctor paused beside Donovan. As he was about to strip off the blanket he noticed Rags lying motionless at the sergeant's feet.

"What in thunder——?" he demanded. Then he took a closer look at the terrier. Rags was in luck. This man liked dogs; understood them. He picked Rags up, turned him this way and that, examined the dressings, and then, puzzled, called an orderly.

"How'd this dog get here," he inquired, "and how'd he get in this condition?"

The ambulance men had broadcast the story of Rags, and of the "orders from headquarters" covering his case. It had spread quickly among the members of the hospital staff. The orderly repeated it to the surgeon. Donovan stirred and murmured:

"Good ol' Rags! He must have made it."

The doctor fished a magnifying glass from his pocket. He examined the injury under Rags's eye, and with a tweezers deftly removed the shell sliver.

"Poor little puppy!" he muttered. "He'll be blind in that eye, but, at that, I think he'll pull through. Terriers are hard to kill."

Instructing the stretcher men to see that Rags and Donovan were not separated, the doctor moved to the next case. Rags was left on the stretcher, undisturbed, while Donovan was lifted to the operating-table. With Donovan after the surgeon had finished, the terrier was passed on. The men who carried them repeated the "orders from headquarters." At Dombasle, the rail-head, the ambulance men made the train commander aware of the "orders." Donovan and Rags got a bottom berth in the triple-deck cots in which the wounded were stowed.

For each carload of wounded there was only one nurse. To give any of the men individual care was impossible. Such food as there was came from the kitchen car, on the front end of the train. By the time it had been carried back, any appetizing qualities it might have possessed had departed. This made little difference to the wounded. Most of them were too sick to care about food. The nurse caught such naps as she could between feeding a little lukewarm broth to men who complained of hunger and giving a hypodermic to those whose pain had become unbearable. For two days and nights they rode the train, sometimes crawling snail-like, now and then sidetracked for munitions expresses, and at intervals tearing along at top speed to clear the track for troops and supplies. The nurse, a kindly, motherly woman, did what she could for Rags. She forced a little broth down his throat, adjusted his dressings, and found an extra pillow for him to lie on. He opened his eyes wearily, moved his tail weakly in gratitude, and then relapsed into inertia. Rags was a very sick dog. Donovan, in mild delirium, murmured over and over again the story of sending the message through.

The morning of the third day was dawning when the train pulled into an improvised station. The wounded men were lifted to the platform, in a drizzling mist, to await their turns in the ambulances. There was the usual protest from the ambulance men against transporting Rags. The medical officer in charge of the train brushed aside their objections.

"Orders from headquarters," he snapped, "and you'd better see that they are carried out."

They did. As soon as they arrived at the quaint old monastery which was being used as a hospital, they passed the information to the commanding officer.

"Orders from headquarters, sir," they explained, "we were instructed to inform you."

To the hospital commander "headquarters" meant John J. Pershing, General of the Armies. In spite of the fact no written orders concerning Rags had reached him, the officer took no chances. General Pershing, he reasoned, probably wouldn't bother to write an order concerning a dog, but would expect his verbal instructions to be carried out. Rags was given a special cot, made out of a packing-case, and permitted to make his home under Donovan's bed. The hospital commander hunted up a veterinary who was his friend, and obtained instructions for the care of the dog.

As the days rolled by Rags began to show signs of convalescence. His appetite revived. Although he made no effort to seek, food, he no longer refused it. Toward the end of his second week in the hospital he came limpingly out from his "cave" under the sergeant's cot and looked pensively up to find out how Donovan was getting on. The ward nurse, a kindly soul, lifted him gently so that he could see his friend. Donovan, still a critical case, brightened at sight of the terrier.

He moved a bandaged arm toward Rags, but the nurse checked him and placed the dog beside him on the bed where he could reach its head without effort. The sergeant scratched Rags's head and murmured:

"Good ol' Rags. You made it all right, didn't you?"

Rags wagged his tail with more energy than he had shown since being wounded, and gave a weak little bark—which the nurse quickly hushed.

"They'll put you out if you make noise," she warned him.

"Just tell him to hush up, ma'am," Donovan whispered. "He's smart an' he'll understand."

Rags understood. His recovery became rapid, and by the day the Armistice was signed he was, in spite of his blind eye, a stone-deaf ear, a bit of a cough, and a slight limp, which seemed most pronounced on rainy days, as spry and chipper as if nothing had happened to him. But he moved around the ward as quietly as a mouse, save for the soft pad-pad of his paws as he hurried in and out. Now that he was able to get around, his passion for exploration gripped him. He ranged over the old

48

monastery from the kitchens of the hospital staff to the office of the commandant, making friends wherever he went.

The monks had selected an ideal site for their home. There was a little stream flowing through the grounds, and hills on either side. In spite of the war-broken men it sheltered, the whole atmosphere of the place was that of an oasis of peace. In the shade of a little wood that monks had nurtured and preserved through the centuries, hares and pigeons ranged. Rags, as his strength returned, got no end of fun chasing both. Yet, it was the minnows swimming in the little stream that fascinated him. The terrier would stand on the bank and watch them, whimpering as if in challenge to them to come up on the land. But the minnows would continue to swim placidly about, not in the least disturbed by the terrier's barks of disapproval.

Watching Rags's feud with the fish became one of the favorite pastimes of those officers and nurses who happened to be off duty. Invariably, after he had scolded them for a time, Rags made up his mind to do something about it. He would dive into the stream, catch no fish, come up panting for breath, wringing wet, and shake himself over the immaculate uniforms of nurses and doctors. They enjoyed his antics and encouraged his fishing activities. It was the catching of a fish that cured Rags of his Ike Walton habits. He had dived in, as usual, but when he landed in the water, an eel was passing. The eel, frightened at the unusual disturbance, twisted itself around Rags. An officer waded into the stream and saved Rags from drowning. Rags had caught his first—and last— fish. The eel, baked to a turn by a French chef expert in such matters, graced the commandant's table that night. Rags gave up fishing.

The hospital command, after taking over the monastery, had carefully tended the monks' flock of goats. The milk was a priceless diet for the desperately wounded. The animals ranged in a pasture on the side of a hill, south of the monastery buildings. Until he became cured of fishing, Rags never had investigated this pasture. But with fishing "all washed up" after his adventure with the eel, Rags resumed exploring and, of course, found the goats. At his bark, half a dozen of them ran off, frightened. An old Billy lifted his head, glared at Rags for a moment, then charged. The terrier was puzzled. Never before, when he barked, had four-footed things defied him. This funny-looking creature with curving horns and a long chin whisker decidedly was not afraid of him. Rags was so amazed that he side-stepped barely in time—and learned something about goats. A charging Billy travels in a straight line.

The goat, realizing, after a run of fifty yards or so that he had missed the dog, halted, glanced around, located Rags, and charged again. This time Rags surprised Billy. He side-stepped adroitly as the goat dashed past, then leaped deftly and fastened his teeth in the animal's whiskers. The sudden weight forward threw the old Billy off his balance and dog and goat rolled over and over on the sod of the pasture. When the goat undertook to get up, Rags was clinging to his whiskers. So once again they rolled around, the goat trying to shake Rags off and Rags refusing to be shaken. An orderly, come to milk the goats, finally separated Rags and the guardian of the flock, shooing the dog toward the hospital. Whatever Rags's views might have been on goats, he had learned that one got along best by obliging men in the olive drab of the American army. So, with a few parting remarks to the old goat he departed.

Back at hospital Rags found a new source of annoyance—a cat. The feline enemy, apparently, had turned up in his absence. It was a beautiful Persian, how it arrived is one of the bright sidelights of an epic of tragedy. The head nurse in Donovan's ward was a dainty slip of a woman. Her hair snow white, her features classic, she might have stepped out of a painting. The story was that her only son—a captain— had fallen at Chateau-Thierry. She lavished all of the love, kindness, and understanding of a true mother on the wounded men who were brought to her ward. All of them, after they had been there a day or two, if they could talk at all, called her "MOTHER".

A little French girl had come through the hospital that day, selling cats. And the patients who were well enough to understand what it was all about, and had managed to retain a few francs, purchased the best one as a gift to "Mother." The cat was curled up under Donovan's bed when Rags arrived. Ten seconds later it was in the arms of "Mother," with Rags on the floor at her feet, begging her to be reasonable and let him get at that cat.

"Why, Rags, I'm ashamed of you!" she chided, holding the cat aloft. "A big, brave soldier like you picking on a poor little kitty. Kitty wouldn't hurt you.'"

Rags tucked his tail between his legs. "Mother" had fed him with a spoon. He couldn't get her viewpoint on cats, but he understood that somehow, by chasing the cat, he had offended her. Rags never wanted to offend his friends. He lay flat on the floor—in all humility—and did his best, with vibration of tail, to express his regret.

"Mother" set the cat beside him.

"There," she said, "be a good dog, Rags, and make friends with Kitty. She's a poor little helpless thing and you'll just have to take care of her."

Rags made no move to attack the cat. But he cast a dubious glance upward at "Mother." He understood that, for some strange reason, he was expected to tolerate this pest.

The cat hissed and spat at him. Then, seeing no hostile move from Rags, she lifted her paw, hit him a mighty clout on the ear, and streaked from the ward. Rags looked after her fast-vanishing form, glanced reproachfully at "Mother," and crawled into his quarters under Donovan's cot.

CHAPTER NINE
HOMEWARD BOUND

DONOVAN did not follow the example of a rapid recovery, set by Rags. His wounds were mending slowly. The intense gassing had almost paralysed his lungs. His vitality was so low that he was unable to gather any reserve force for a fight back to health. Doctors shook their heads solemnly over him. They doubted he ever would be a well man again. Of one thing they were certain—the French climate was no boon to a soldier suffering from lung trouble. Donovan, they decided, must be sent to the United States as soon as possible.

Rags they would have been glad to keep—his friendly ways brightened the hospital—but they felt he should not be separated from Donovan. When the sergeant was placed on the hospital train for Brest, Rags had his old place at the foot of the cot. The train moved much more expeditiously than the one that had brought Rags and Donovan from Dombasle. The war was over. No longer were hospital trains delayed while troops and munitions moved. The nursing staff was adequate. Warm food was served at regular intervals. Rags ranged through the coaches, making friends with the men who were able to notice him.

At one of the station stops the terrier struck up an acquaintance with a limping, battered colonel. The office, surprised to find a dog on a hospital train, made inquiries and learned Rags's history.

"H'm!" he grunted. "I've heard of him. He's the little pup that took a message through a barrage. Donovan was in my company during his first hitch, Fine soldier! Good little dog!"

He scratched Rags's neck and head in just the right places, and before the train pulled out made certain the dog was back aboard.

At Brest there was a conglomerate collection of vehicles to transport the casuals to the ship. Some soldiers, almost well, rode busses and cabs. Others, physically whole, but suffering from shell-shock, climbed trucks. The more seriously sick, Donovan among them, were placed in ambulances. Rags selected his accustomed place at Donovan's feet. But the ambulance men—replacements who had arrived since the fighting had stopped, who never had heard of Rags—unceremoniously pushed him aside and drove away. So the terrier trotted over the rough paving in the wake of the ambulance until it reached the dock. There, with tongue lolling excitedly, he watched them carry Donovan aboard. When he tried to follow he ran against the stone wall of regulations, which forbade pets of any sort on hospital ships. Several of his friends pleaded for him, but were curtly informed that only one man in all Europe had authority to make exceptions to the order—General Pershing. Too late they remembered the formula that had won Rags's way to the base hospital— "Orders from headquarters."

Rags knew. He was a pathetic little figure, still gamely watching for a chance to get aboard, when the colonel he had met on the train came along. The officer sized up the situation at a glance. He wasted no time in argument.

"See that dog, Bill?" he told his orderly. "The little tan terrier?"

"Yes, sir."

"That's Donovan's dog—the one that carried that message through."

"Yes, sir. I soldiered with Donovan in the colonel's company."

"Good. Take the stuff out of my handbag and stick it in your pack. Put the dog in the bag and get him aboard."

"Very good, sir."

Nobody presumed to inspect the colonel's luggage, and Rags soon found himself in an airy deck cabin, being hush-hushed and ordered to remain still. He crawled under the bunk and made no sound. Soon he was asleep. When he awakened the ship was under way.

The colonel, moving about, bossing the placing of his luggage, grinned a welcome when Rags crawled from under the bunk.

"You're smart, all right," he told the terrier as he scratched the spots that Rags offered for attention. "As soon as we get on the other side I'm going to have something done about those fleas of yours, if I can find a vet."

Rags wagged his tail and set himself for a grateful bark. The colonel looked him squarely in the eye.

"None o' that, now," he admonished. "I don't suppose they'd throw you overboard, but some dumb idiot might prefer charges against me. Shut up and keep quiet."

Rags sat thumping his tail. He was grateful to the colonel, but there was a restless uneasiness in his manner. He was, obviously, concerned about Donovan. The colonel understood.

"Your friend's all right," he explained. "You'd like to see him? Well, you'll have to wait. You're a stowaway, old-timer, and you'd better remember it. Just stay hidden under my bunk, if you don't want to make a lot of trouble for us. Come, now!"

The colonel shooed Rags under the berth and made the terrier understand he would have to keep out of sight.

"Remarkable breed, terriers," the officer to his orderly. "Boss 'em around and they pay no attention to you. Make them understand there's a good reason for doing something, and they are almost human."

"Yes, sir," the orderly concurred. "I've noticed, already, that the minute I start to open the door he runs under your bunk and stays there until he finds out who it is."

"I wish I could ease his mind and let him know Donovan is aboard," the colonel murmured. "It's a pity to have the poor little fellow so worried."

"If the colonel would permit a suggestion?" the orderly began.

"Shoot!"

"Donovan was in the colonel's company army. It would be natural for you to want to visit him. You could wrap the dog in your overcoat and take him along. Nurses and officers aren't very snappy late in the evening, and they wouldn't pay any attention if the colonel had his overcoat wadded up under his arm."

"Good idea, Bill."

On the second night out the colonel limped about the decks until he located Donovan's Cot. While most of the patients were in three-deck beds, Donovan had been allotted the bottom cot on a two-decker, an indication he was regarded as a critical case. The colonel went to his quarters, carefully wrapped Rags in his overcoat, and issued an emphatic warning.

"No yelping, now," he told Rags. "I'm taking you to see your friend, but one yip out of you and we're both sunk. You're to be seen, not heard. Understand? Keep quiet."

Rags nestled in the folds of the colonel's coat and scarcely breathed. The officer shuffled about—shivering a bit in the chill wind, with the coat crumpled under his arm. After he had satisfied himself he was arousing no suspicion he edged painfully through the bays until he came to Donovan.

As he stood beside the bed he admonished Rags, with a pressure of his elbow, to be quiet.

Donovan was tossing restlessly. He failed to recognize in the lined, pain-racked features of the colonel, the fresh-faced young company commander he had known, as a rookie, in the Philippines.

"How're you feeling, boy?" the colonel asked.

"Rotten, sir. Don't seem able to catch my breath regular."

"Friend o' yours here wants to see you. Don't get him stirred up.

He's a stowaway; but he's been wantin' to check up on you."

Puzzled, Donovan glanced up at the colonel. The officer placed his bundled coat on the bed.

"Don't you go giving any cheers, either. Rags has been right worried about you. I think he'll feel better after he knows you're aboard."

Carefully watching for nurses and orderlies, the colonel unwound the coat so Rags could get his head out. The terrier licked Donovan's face. The sergeant cautioned him,

"Be quiet now, you!"

Rags made no sound. Donovan, at length, weakly pushed him back into the folds of the colonel's great-coat.

"Thanks, Colonel," the sergeant murmured. "I think I've got a ticket west, but I'd hate to have the pup turned loose on his own again. He's one swell little soldier. The pair of us was through some hot spots."

The colonel brushed a couple of tears from his eyes. He was no sentimentalist. Ten thousand men, who now and then had come under his command, had voted him "hard boiled." Perhaps not more than half of them would have admitted he was human.

"I'll try and see you're not separated," he promised as he carried Rags away. "In fact, I'll get Rags on the same train with you."

As he carried the dog below the colonel sensed something unusual aboard the ship. Guard details were passing from one ward to another, looking for something.

"Guess they know you're aboard," he whispered to Rags, "so you'd better be extra still. Get yourself behind that trunk under my bed and don't move. Understand?"

It would seem Rags did. Assurance Donovan was on the boat apparently had satisfied him. He was perfectly amenable to the colonel's suggestion. He made it plain that he understood that only the colonel, his orderly, and Donovan could be trusted with the information Rags was aboard. As he hid himself behind the colonel's locker-trunk there was a knock on the stateroom door. The orderly opened it.

A couple of white-clad men stood outside.

"We've come to search the colonel's quarters," one of them announced. "A sailor brought a cat aboard and it's loose somewhere. We're looking for it."

The colonel's hesitation lasted scarcely a fraction of a second. Then his indignation burst forth—real, intense and formidable.

"Search my quarters!" he roared. "Who the devil aboard this boat thinks he has authority to search my quarters. Get out of here!"

"But if the colonel pleases," one of the men spoke up, "the chief medical officer is afraid the cat will spread germs. We've got to find it."

"Find it, then," shouted the colonel, "but don't you dare come around here again bothering me."

He swung the door shut. The men outside waited a moment and went away. The colonel did a little fast thinking. He talked to Rags.

"You stay here, mister," he advised. "Don't stick your head out until you are called."

The dog scarcely heeded him. The ship was pitching heavily. Rags was not a good sailor. He was seasick. The colonel pulled him out, examined him, and chuckled.

"You'll get better—and you're not likely to do much frolicking, the way you feel."

He dug a blanket and a poncho out of his bags, placed the poncho on top of the blanket and made a comfortable bed for Rags. Then he limped up on the deck and sought the medical officer. He was making certain there would be no more invasions of his quarters. The medical commander was apologetic. He had not intended that the colonel's quarters be searched. Besides, the cat had been found, had been chloroformed, and was no longer a basis for argument. The colonel, feeling better, went below. He decided it was just as well Rags was sick. After all, the medical officer was boss of the ship. Probably he'd be no more considerate of the terrier than he had been of the cat.

"Keep Rags out of sight, Bill," the colonel told his orderly, "until we see the old lady with the torch."

"Very good, sir," Bill agreed. "I'll sure be glad to see her."

"You an' me both; I'll be glad to get the dog on his way. I promised Donovan."

The passage continued rough. Rags showed little interest in his surroundings. It was not until the hospital ship slipped into New York Harbor that the terrier regained his poise. Then, as the boat passed the Statue of Liberty, he showed a desire to go exploring. The colonel promptly talked him out of that.

"You'll stay right where you are until we get to Hoboken," the colonel warned. "When you get on land again you can prowl around to your heart's content."

There was a delay in docking. For several hours the hospital ship lay at anchor while officers were finding a pier at which to berth it, and making up a train. The colonel got Rags ashore in the same handbag that had carried him aboard. Then he sent Bill, the orderly, to make discreet inquiries, to find if Rags could be smuggled aboard the hospital train with Donovan. Bill's report was encouraging.

At the railhead in Hoboken two trains were being made up: one to carry surgical cases to the Walter Reed Hospital in Washington, the other to take shell-shock and gas patients to Fort Sheridan, near Chicago. The colonel was ticketed for the Walter Reed treatment, because of his leg injuries. Donovan, listed as a gas case, was assigned to Fort Sheridan. Bill found several old comrades who, although suffering shell-shock or gas, were well enough to move around. These were bound for the same destination as Donovan. They would guarantee to see that Rags and Donovan were reunited at the end of the trip. The only difficulty would be getting Rags on the train.

The colonel, checking over the names of Bill's friends, found several soldiers who had served under him. To these, he decided, he would bid farewell, carrying Rags as he had carried him to Donovan's cot aboard the ship. Because of his wounds, the officer had difficulty in getting up the steps of the car. With the help of Bill and a nurse he managed it. Rags snuggled in the colonel's great-coat, still as a mouse. Aboard the train the terrier was pushed under a berth and cautioned to be silent. He showed no disposition to be otherwise. There was a light of understanding in his one good eye as the colonel scratched his neck and voiced a farewell warning.

"In a couple of days," the officer told Rags, "you can range and romp to your heart's content. But be still here."

Rags tail moved almost furtively. He licked the colonel's hand.

"He know we're keeping him near Donovan," the officer explained to the dog's guardians. "I'm convinced he understands perfectly that he has to stay hidden."

Rags made it plain that he did. On the entire trip he made no sound. He moved only to eat the light ration and drink the water his custodians slipped under the berth to him. Not even the jarring of the cars, as engines were changed, and again as the train was shunted through various yards, caused the terrier to quit his cramped quarters. At times he dozed fitfully. Whenever one of his guardians peered under the berth the dog would cock his head to one side and focus his good eye inquiringly on the soldier, as if expecting to be bidden out. Receiving only a friendly pat and a renewed caution to be quiet and still, he made no move.

As the train neared Fort Sheridan the terrier's custodians held conference. To take the dog off openly, they decided, meant being accused of breaking regulations. It would be better, they agreed, to smuggle him off. When the train rolled gently to a stop on one of the Fort Sheridan sidings Rags was called out of his "cave". An overcoat was spread on the berth. Its owner stooped to lift the dog. Rags anticipated him. After a quick glance from the coat to its owner terrier hopped on the berth and settled himself down to be camouflaged.

As the soldier stepped off the train, a young medical officer who was supervising the unloading noticed the overcoat crumpled under the man's arm.

"Put that coat on!" he snapped. "Want to get pneumonia?"

Rags's guardian was nonplused for the moment. Another member of the "Rags committee" did some fast thinking. He stepped around behind the officer and asked a question.

"Will the captain let me go into town to see some friends?" he inquired.

The officer wheeled. In about fifty explosive words he said "No!"

When he turned back to continue his rebuke of the coatless one that soldier had melted, with Rags, into the crowd of stretcher men, soldiers and casuals, clustered around the train.

CHAPTER TEN
THE IMMIGRANT

RAGS'S escort pushed his way through soldiers who were waiting to carry the stretcher cases to the big temporary hospital; through the medical men who were bossing them; through the hospital cases who were able to walk; through the soldiers who had come down to see the train unloaded. Locating Donovan's stretcher he cautiously set Rags on the ground beside it. The terrier raised himself up to see how Donovan was getting on, but a stretcher-bearer pushed him away. Rags stood back, but kept his good eye on the stretcher, and followed it when it moved. At the hospital entrance they barred him. He had run into that before and it didn't discourage him particularly

Meanwhile, the new arrivals at the post were spreading the story of the soldier and the dog who together had carried a message through at the Meuse-Argonne. While Rags was scouting around the hospital, getting a line on the chances of sneaking in, a large delegation of the post population was moving on the hospital for a look at Rags. The terrier located and tried the several entrances without success. A couple of medical officers came along just as the dog settled himself cannily by the main door, awaiting his chance to slip in.

From the descriptions they had heard they recognized him as the Meuse-Argonne hero. Knowing and liking dogs themselves, they sensed at once he wanted to see Donovan. So they took him in. Rags paid his respects to Donovan. Then, satisfied his friend was in good hands, he set about to explore the Fort Sheridan reservation. It was far more extensive than the old monastery grounds. It had much more timber. It lacked the little stream, but Lake Michigan lapped one edge of it. Rags had no further taste for fishing, but he stood for a time watching the play of the waves. It was well after noon when he returned to the hospital. Waiting expectantly until some one came along to him in, he was rebuffed twice. This situation was different from the one in France. Rags waited for third rebuff and started away. He was hungry, and on his early tour of the post had detected the smell of cooking from several quarters. He presented himself at the first mess kitchen that offered. The cook's police fed him as a matter of course.

His hunger satisfied, Rags returned to the conquest of the hospital. Luck was with him. Pleasant officers who had learned about him let him in to Donovan again. He took no chances on going out and not getting back, but concealed himself under the sergeant's cot until after dusk. Hungry again, he slipped down the corridor to the door. A surprised nurse let him out—almost shooed him out. He selected a different mess kitchen for his evening meal. It was late and the kitchen crew was putting the finishing touches to its night clean-up. Hurrying to get through, they fixed up a quick lunch for Rags, piled a few old bags in a corner to make him a bed, locked him in, and went their way. It was after midnight when an officer heard Rags barking and let him out. The terrier hurried to the hospital but could find no one to let him in.

He waited for a time. There was a cold drizzle, driven like a needle bath by a chill wind off the lake. Rags had imbibed some of the prejudice of the soldier by staying out in inclement weather when shelter might be had. Probably the chill dampness was affecting his wounded leg. He left the front of the darkened hospital and made a swing past the barracks, officers' quarters, and other buildings. All were unlighted and forbidding. Far down the main post street Rags noticed a gleam and headed for it. It came from the post fire-house, where the members of the night fire-guard detail dozed or played cards. One of the doors had been left slightly ajar for ventilation. Rags could not quite squeeze through. He put his face close to the opening and barked. One of the soldiers let him in. All of them wanted to play with him—to see if he knew any tricks, and if not, to teach him some. The terrier, however, was in no mood for play. He shook the rain from his coat, crawled under the hose cart and went to sleep.

In the morning he was up and gone, foraging for his breakfast. Then he took up his station at the hospital entrance and waited. Eventually he got in. The rest of his day was a parallel to the day before. Denied admission to the hospital at night, he sought shelter in the fire-house. For some reason he preferred his "cave" under the hose cart to softer resting-places offered elsewhere.

Within a few months he had established at Fort Sheridan in much the same position he enjoyed at the old monastery. He was free to come and go in the daytime, and was permitted to lie alongside but not under Donovan's cot. At night he was barred. It was a long time before he gave up trying to make a night visit, and in that period the fire-house became a habit with him. At the hospital people grew more tolerant, having come to realize that Rags could be trusted to cause no disturbance, and he spent more and more of his days with the sergeant. Donovan seemed brighter, making a better fight to get well, when Rags was around. Naturally, when compelled to be so still and quiet, the terrier dozed a great deal. He took his exercise at night, exploring every corner of the reservation, and always ending up at the fire-house.

His acquaintanceship on the post broadened. Eventually everybody came to know him and to point with pride to the post's possession of a dog with a war record. The commanding officer bought him a collar with a lock. The collar had "First Division Rags" on it. The commander kept the key, as custodian for Donovan, who, it was held, was the trustee of the division in the matter of Rags. Rags displayed no immediate gratitude for the gift. He tried to paw it off. In the end he became resigned, as he did to most things. Life settled into routine for him; daily visits to Donovan, regular rounds of the various messes; exploration and exercise in the evening and return to the fire-house at night.

Once, on an early trip to supper, Rags happened along as the sunset gun boomed and the flag was coming down. Everybody was standing at the salute. The terrier proved that his memory of war days still was keen. He stopped in his tracks, stiffened, and lifted his right paw. Soldiers who noticed carried the news to the fire-house. The men of the fire detail, proud of the prestige gained by what they regarded as a trick, set out to teach Rags others. The terrier walked out of the fire-house. He did not return until the fire detail changed. Coaxing had no effect on him. Nobody ever found out where he put in his nights that week. But he visited Donovan as usual. Other attempts to induce him to perform fared no better. He would sit up and ask for food; he would stand at attention' when soldiers stood at attention; he would salute when they did. That was all. In the end he was left in peace.

Rags's life was as regular as that of any soldiers on the post when Donovan took a turn for the worse. The sergeant seemed to be sleeping most of the time when Rags was with him. The terrier took on a wistful look. Sometimes he would stand by the cot and whimper softly. Getting no response from Donovan, he would lie down again and wait. He missed meals and took on an underfed, unkempt look. But it was not until Donovan was taken to the "critical" ward that the terrier appeared to be really ill. Refused admittance, he would return to the fire-house and mope for a few hours, then make another attempt to enter hospital.

"The little fellow knows Donovan's goin' west," one of the fire detail remarked, while Rags was musing under the hose-cart. The terrier lifted his head, fixed his good eye on the speaker, then got up and hurried from the place. He made another to get into the hospital. Failing, he returned to the fire-house, but, in a few hours he was again making a reconnaissance. Rags was not the dog to give up while he was able to move at all. In the end his gameness was rewarded. An officer, to whom Rags, after many rebuffs, had ceased to appeal—although away from the hospital the man was friendly—came hurrying toward the entrance. Rags hid around the corner and then stole softly at the officer's heels. Not having seen the terrier, the officer didn't bother to push the door shut behind him. He let it swing with the door-check. In the few seconds of delay Rags was inside. He slunk along the corridor from shadow to shadow until he saw a chance to dodge into the ward where he had last seen Donovan. In spite of his hunger weakness he was under the nearest bed in a flash. From that he slipped under another, and still others until he came to the cot that had been Donovan's.

When his nose told him another was in the cot he gave a peculiar moan. Quickly he investigated the remaining beds in the ward—still furtive as a cat. Baffled at the end, he moaned again. Moans were no novelty in the ward. Rags's might have passed unnoticed had he not abandoned his secrecy. But as soon as he satisfied himself that Donovan was not there he came out of his hiding and walked dejectedly down the middle of the ward. Nurses and orderlies saw him and hastened toward him to speed his departure. They feared the censure of the chief medical officer if the dog's presence came to his notice. But Rags never quickened his pace. Instead, he halted, faced about and focused his good eye on them. There was no suggestion of hostility in the movement; no snarl nor growl. It wasn't even swift. The terrier merely turn slowly, almost painfully, and conveyed by a look and a gesture his resentment and reproach. The would be bouncers stood where they had halted when Rags faced them. For perhaps half a minute the tableau lasted. Then Rags turned about again and slowly continued his way out of the ward and down the corridor to the door. There he waited patiently for some one him out.

The chief medical officer finally obliged him. Always in the past Rags had paused long enough to express thanks to those who helped him. This time he walked through the door with slow, dragging steps, and without a single pause or a glance behind, continued on his way to the fire-house. A kindly man, and a friend of dogs, especially an admirer of the little terrier, the chief medical officer made a few discreet inquiries and learned how Rags had searched the ward. He discovered, too, from the fire-house detail, that the terrier seemed to be grieving himself sick. With all the evidence in, as it were, he made up his mind that regulations or no regulations, he would take Rags to see Donovan in the critical ward the next day. That night Donovan's gas-torn lungs gave out. The sergeant joined his comrades in Valhalla.

The chief medical officer himself next morning regretfully carried the news to the fire-house. He explained his good intentions of the night before and wondered if something couldn't be done to halt the decline of Rags. A young rookie from the west, who had been raised with all sorts of dogs, ventured a suggestion.

"I think, sir," he said, "that if Rags could be made to understand that his pal had gone west, he'd be all right. Terriers are a queer lot. Probably what worries his most is the feeling that Sergeant Donovan is thinking he's deserted him."

"How're you going to tell him?" the officer inquired, a bit impatiently. "He can't talk."

"Terriers are smart, sir. I'm sure if Rags saw the cot he sergeant had last he'd understand."

"Pick him up and follow me."

The soldier obeyed. After explaining to the sergeant in charge of the fire detail, the medical officer led the way toward the hospital. Beside the cot that had been Donovan's they paused.

"Tell him if you can," the officer commanded.

"The soldier placed the terrier on the cot. He spoke almost in a whisper, extending his hands in a gesture of despair.

"Donovan's gone west, Rags," he explained. "You won't see him any more. Gone west!"

Rags moaned and whimpered, but so lowly that the men scarcely heard him. He sniffed, stretched himself, with forepaws extended and nose buried between them, and lay motionless for more than a minute. Then, without another sound, he jumped off the bed and moved toward the exit. The men followed.

"He feels pretty badly, sir," the soldier explained. "He'll mope for a day or two. Then I think he'll get over it. Terriers are pretty game."

"I hope he gets over it," the officer murmured.

Rags waited for them to open the outer door. Once outside, in contrast to his conduct of the day before, he paused, looked up at them, and wagged his tail. Then, standing politely to one side until they had passed, he made his way to the fire-house. For a week he moped, more or less, but gradually resumed regular eating. Little by little he began visiting his old haunts—the various messes, the officers' club, the stables. He never went near the hospital again. It became noticeable that he would make a detour to avoid it.

CHAPTER ELEVEN
A NEW FRIENDSHIP

THE year following Donovan's death saw many changes at Fort Sheridan. Officers came and went. Outfits moved out and were replaced. Rags stayed on. He lodged at the fire-house and took his meals where his fancy led him. Company messes, officers' club, the kitchens of the married officers were all on his visiting-list. Rags knew just what sort of table every officer in the garrison set; whether their cook was good or bad; and indeed whether a cook was maintained or the food prepared by the mistress of the household. No sooner did a new officer get settled than Rags drifted around and inspected the family's culinary arrangements. This little eccentricity of his became one of the big laughs of the post. Newcomers were immediately informed of it. So, when Rags appeared, they knew something of his history and accorded him hospitality. Just the same, many a young wife, caught in her kitchen in her morning dishabille, was glad the terrier couldn't talk; some of the prim and nosy ladies wished that he could.

Among the new arrivals at the post was Major R. W Hardenbergh and his family, which included two vivacious little daughters, Helen, fifteen years old, and her sister Sue, seven.

Rags, as was his habit, dropped in and looked over their kitchen as soon as they were settled. He given a pleasant welcome, and, apparently satisfied, went his way. They saw no more of him, for a time. Officers were moving in and Rags was busy looking them over.

The Hardenbergh sisters started attending school at Winnetka, the nearest town which had adequate educational facilities. To reach it they had to travel several miles by interurban train, which passed through the post a considerable distance from the major's quarters. The girls rode their bicycles from home to the fire-house, and left them there, riding them again when they returned from school. Rags was not at his lodgings the first day the children started for school. But he was there when they returned in the afternoon and he started to get acquainted without the formality of an introduction. The children, frightened, hopped on their bicycles and pedaled as fast as they could go. Arriving home, they told their father the fearsome tale of the great big dog that had chased them.

The major had a rare understanding of dogs. He listened to the story, asked a few questions, divided the alleged size of the dog by about three, and decided Rags was the culprit. Then he laughed.

"Don't be afraid of him," he advised. "That's only Rags, the post dog. He wouldn't hurt a fly."

He recounted the story of the dog's exploits, but this didn't reassure the children. Rags might be friendly with flies, they opined, but his attitude toward little girls had been decidedly hostile.

To everybody except the children it was plain that Rags was bent on making friends. He barked his most melodious bark, wagged his tail as if he was going to shake it completely off, and pranced toward them in his most ingratiating manner. But still the children were afraid. After half a dozen attempts to get acquainted Rags appeared to realize what was wrong. When the girls next came for their bicycles he remained motionless and silent under the hose-cart. Nor did he move when they departed. In the morning when they came and left their bicycles he made no advances. In the afternoon, when they returned, he was not there. The children were rather glad. Maybe, they told other, he wouldn't bother them any more. They didn't know Rags.

The wily terrier had taken up a post down the road they regularly traveled, and, concealed in the weeds, watched for their arrival. When they passed him on their bicycles, pedaling slowly, now that the "ferocious dog" wasn't chasing them, he stalked them through his cover, and carefully marked the house into which they went. Once the children were inside, Rags hurried around to the back door and renewed his acquaintance with the cook. He wasn't hungry, so he nibbled daintily and lingered. Soon little Sue, hungry after her day in school, came dancing in the kitchen for a snack before dinner. Rags made no advances. He busied himself with his food, but watched her warily out of his good eye. The fear the child felt when she met the terrier at the fire-station vanished as she found him in her own home. She ran over to him and patted his head and scratched his back. Rags submitted passively. She rubbed him a bit harder, with the heel of her shoe—in all friendliness—and Rags acknowledged the attention with a wag of his tail. Then she called him by name and told him he was a "nice doggie."

Rags got to his feet, tail vibrating like a big, fuzzy tuning fork, and almost bowed. He sat up and lifted his paws, a gesture he seldom made. She gave him a big hug then and ran to call her sister. Helen, a bit skeptical, was duly introduced. Soon she was petting the dog as fondly as Sue. The terrier frolicked with them until they were called to prepare for dinner. Rags took no chances of wearing out his welcome. As soon as the children left the kitchen he went back to the fire-house. But a wonderful friendship had been started.

Before breakfast, next morning, Rags was on the Hardenberghs' back porch. As soon as he finished his meal, he hurried around to the front and waited for the children to start for school. They greeted him with cries of delight, petted him, and, mounting their bicycles, began a race with him to the fire-house. Racing was not Rags's forte, in view of his wounds, but he did his best to keep up. The children were kind, however, and when he got a little behind, slowed down and waited for him. After they parked their bicycles at the fire-house Rags gleefully escorted them to the station. They had difficulty in convincing him that he couldn't go on the train. When they returned that night, Rags, who had been watching, went hurrying down the road to meet them. Children and dog raced home as they had raced to the fire-house in the morning.

When the party reached the Hardenbergh home, Rags started around toward the back door, with a sort of "see you later" look in his eye. The children grabbed him and led him, almost protesting, in the front door. They told the major of how fine and friendly Rags was, how he had come to meet them, and how he had raced with them home. Also, they announced they wanted to keep him.

The major chuckled. He explained that Rags was a member of the army, as it were, and that no individual could lay any claim to him. He advised against too deep an attachment, because, if the Hardenberghs left the post, they could not, in view of Rags status, take him along. In the meantime, he told them, if Rags wanted to board and lodge with them he was welcome.

Rags wanted to do just that. He danced with glee when they led him to the kitchen for supper, but when the children bade him good night and started for bed, he politely moved toward the door. The major was pleased and amused as Rags stood patiently waiting to be let out.

"Knows enough to go home," he commentated, "which is more than can be said for some humans."

Hunting up an old blanket, the major folded it and fixed a bed for Rags in a corner. He called Rags, pointed to it, and said, "Lie down, Rags." Then he opened the door. The terrier stood doubtfully on the threshold. The major called him again and pointed to the blanket. Rags walked across the room, barked his thanks, and curled up on the blanket. He never slept in the fire-house again.

Each day the terrier saw the children off to school and met them on their return. If they were at play around the post, Rags was at their heels. Except for romping with them, he never played any regular games; nor did the children trouble him by trying to teach him tricks. They were proud of his war record and satisfied with his loyalty. It became a maxim around the garrison that if one saw the dog the children were either somewhere near him, or else absent from the post. Rags still retained his friendships by industrious visiting in the hours when the children were at school. He took luncheon at a different place each day, until he made the rounds. Then he started over again. But for breakfast and dinner he was always on hand at the Hardenbergh home. Gradually the garrison forgot that Rags was a veteran with whose care the entire post was charged. It was taken for granted he belonged to the Hardenberghs.

When the major was ordered to Camp Benning, Georgia, the status of Rags became a matter of official concern. Major Hardenbergh regretfully explained to the children that Rags could not go along—he was a ward of the Fort Sheridan garrison. And the major, as an officer, could not ask the post to turn its trusteeship over to him. Such things just weren't done. The children couldn't see it that way at all. They "went politician," as the saying is, and canvassed all of the influential persons on the post, not overlooking the commandant. Their argument was sound; none ventured to challenge it. Rags had been virtually homeless until he had adopted them, and, they pointed out, it wasn't fair to make him homeless again. Everybody had tried to win his friendship; nobody had succeeded in getting beyond the casual acquaintanceship Rags displayed for all soldiers. He had selected the Hardenberghs himself, and with some difficulty at that. The justice of the claim was admitted and a post council was called. By unanimous vote the major and the children were declared trustees of Rags in so far as the post council had authority to declare it. The commandant formally turned over to Major Hardenbergh the key to Rags's collar. It was a happy arrangement for all concerned, although the members of the garrison hated to see Rags go. There was, understanding that, if Rags elected to remain at the post, he would not be compelled to leave.

Rags quickly dispelled any doubts as to his attentions. As soon as the symptoms of moving appeared he recognized them. When the major moved about, giving instructions for the packing, Rags remained with him, looking up every now and then, and saying as plainly as if he had spoken:

"You're going to take me too, I hope."

From the day he noticed the preparation for travel Rags never permitted the entire family to get out of his sight at once. Always he kept his eye on at least one member of it. When the family finally got into the car that was to take them to the train, Rags hopped in without waiting for an invitation. The children hugged him and petted him and assured him that there would be no permanent separation. At the railroad station the major produced a leash, the first Rags ever had worn, and hooked it to the terrier's collar. The terrier looked at it over his shoulder disapprovingly, but made no further protest.

Rags headed for the Pullmans—they resembled the only cars on which he had ever ridden, so he took it for granted that he would ride in one of them now. When the major lifted him into the baggage-car he sat up and pleaded protestingly. The children came back and explained to him, patted him, and coaxed him to submit to being tied up. He looked at them reproachfully when they left, and then stretched himself out, head on paws. His manner was eloquently expressive of the thought that, if these friends deserted him he didn't much care what happened anyhow. He hardly moved until the train pulled into Chicago, where the family transferred to a train for the south. The children hurried back to see the terrier. He brightened even before he saw them, as their hurrying feet pattered along the station platform.

Transferred to the south-bound train, Rags took none of his blue mood with him. The visit at the station had assured him he was going with the family. He appeared to feel that the baggage-car business was just a variation of the concealment that had attended his trip across the ocean and to Fort Sheridan, and settled down to make himself as comfortable as he could. The baggage-car crew took an interest in him. The children had proudly informed them that he was a "real war dog who had been wounded in battle." As had many before them, the trainmen undertook to put Rags through some tricks. Whereupon he turned his tail to them and lay down by the side of the car in an attitude of outraged dignity. The chief baggage-man, who was a British veteran, observed the terrier's action with glee.

"'Tis a bloomin' little sergeant-major 'e is," he told the others. "It's salutin' 'im we'd ought to be."

Suiting the action to the word, the chief raised his hand in a British salute. Rags eyed him for a moment. It wasn't the salute he had known, but he recognized the stiff attention, and scrambled to his feet. Then he assumed his saluting pose, until the baggage-man dropped his hand in sheer astonishment. There were no more attempts to make an entertainer out of Rags. Each baggage crew passed the word along, and its successor contented itself with saluting Rags and being saluted in return. He arrived at Camp Benning rated the world's most distinguished baggage-car passenger.

At camp Benning Rags found many soldiers wearing the insignia of the First Division, but, before he had the chance to get acquainted the family was on the move again. In his new travels Rags visited Washington and Annapolis and finally arrived at Camp Knox, where the major had to look after some Citizens' Military Training Camp students. Rags displayed little interest in the students, although they made a great fuss over him. The terrier was a veteran, used to the company of veterans, and had all the veteran's contempt for the rookie. His attitude all but shouted as much. He accepted their farewells politely when the time came for the major to return to Benning, but he didn't display any enthusiasm.

Back at Benning, Rags began to show openly a fear of which he had only shown symptoms before—he was afraid of automobiles. Members of the garrison began to remark that if there was a single motor-car in sight, Rags would wait until some one came along to escort him across the street. Never, unless a member of the summoned him, would he cross with one of the contraptions where he could see it. He never missed a chance to ride in one, but he almost trembled when one of the things flashed past him in the road. When the residents of the post realized the little terrier's fear, he seldom had to cross alone; usually some one saw him waiting and hurried along to act as Rags's escort.

His fear of the automobiles, however, did not keep him from exploring. Sure of his place with the Hardenberghs, he wandered about, sampling kitchen facilities as of old, making friends wherever he went. Barring the cats and one sulky police dog, Rags didn't have an enemy in the garrison. The police dog didn't like Rags, and made no secret of his enmity. Whenever Rags came in sight the police dog growled and snarled and strained at the chain that held him to the steps of an officer's dwelling. The first time Rags heard the growl he stiffened, faced the hostile dog, and looked him over coolly. On discovering his enemy was tied up Rags ignored him and trotted away. He paid no attention to the challenges after that.

One day the police dog got loose and bore down on Rags, snapping and snarling. He caught the terrier off guard. But Rags met the attack without flinching. He flung himself to one side as quickly as his slightly stiff leg would permit and drew first blood with a slashing jab of his teeth under his assailant's eye. Then Rags pressed the attack, trying for a spine grip. The police dog outweighed him by three to one and shook him off. Rags tried for the throat, but the shaggy mane of his enemy protected that vulnerable spot. Rags took several vicious slashes, and then the police dog got a grip on the terrier's crippled ear. Rags twisted and, without regard for his ear, grabbed the police dog's nose. Then he clung.

Meanwhile everybody in the garrison who heard the noise of the battle hurried to the rescue of Rags. Military police pounded the police dog with their clubs; officers and soldiers kicked one another's shins in an effort to boot Rags's assailant into retreat. The police dog was willing enough to quit, what with all the force against him. But he couldn't leave Rags. The terrier was hanging on like grim death. Not until the second pail of water was splashed over the battlers did Rags release his hold on his enemy's nose. Even then, his fighting blood thoroughly up, Rags started to pursue as soon as he had shaken the water out of his eye. The major had to restrain him by force. It was conceded that Rags, in the long run, couldn't have won. The other dog was too big, and a fighter. But the terrier was willing to try, and his gameness made him more the pet of the garrison than before. The police dog made no further attacks, although occasionally loose. Nor did Rags. The terrier never stepped an inch out of his way for the other dog. If either gave way, it was Rags's enemy. Beyond that neither appeared to see the other.

The family was glad. They appreciated Rags's valor, but they didn't want him risking his life and limb in fights. They were happy, now that he was safe. And just as they had settled into a feeling of security about him, he disappeared. At first they believed he might have wandered off on an exploring tour. But when the second day passed without sign of him a search was ordered. High and low, soldiers and officers, even civilians, hunted for the terrier without success.

The major found him at last—a bloody, broken little bundle, more dead than alive—in the coal bin of the Hardenbergh home. He had been hit by an automobile and almost every bone in his body appeared to have been fractured. The post veterinary was summoned. The children even called the post surgeon. Carefully lifted on a blanket, the terrier was carried upstairs to a cushioned resting-place beside the living room grate. There he lingered for days, lapping a little water, but eating nothing. Through it all not a whimper came from him. At times he was so still the children feared he had "gone west." But when they approached him he would open his good eye and with a painful effort move his tail slightly. Then he would lapse into a coma again. But he never quit for a moment, in his game fight to get well. He mended, at first slowly; then rapidly. When the major was ordered to Plattsburg for the summer Citizens' Military Training Camp, Rags insisted friskily on going along. He was himself again.

CHAPTER TWELVE
A WAR DOG MEETS A RED

AS soon as Rags reached Plattsburg he went exploring.
He seemed to have mellowed a bit. In his Camp Knox days he had "high-hatted" the training-camp rookies. Now he was tolerant of all of them, friendly with many. Frequently he would accompany a group of the youngsters to town. The student soldiers made much of him. When their friends or relatives turned up with pedigreed dogs, the boys would point to Rags and challenge the show dogs to match his record.

There was an undercurrent of trouble for Rags at Plattsburg that year. The so-called "Reds" were making a demonstration against the camp. Rags, through some psychic sense, classified these persons as enemies of his caste—the soldier caste—and conceived an intense hostility for them. It finally burst out one day when he went into the town on the heels of a group of students. These halted at a corner where a man on a soap-box was making a speech. The terrier bristled as soon as the sound of the man's voice.

The terrier bristled as soon as his good ear caught the sound of the man's voice.

"The capitalists," the speaker was shouting, "are training you to be their butchers. Why should you go out and kill your brothers? Stick with your class! Take off the livery of your masters. Don't be a lot of yellow dogs!"

Rags interrupted the speaker with a sharp and disapproving bark. It was as if the dog had understood the contemptuous reference to his own color—olive after all, is a cross between yellow and green. The man, nonplused for a moment, was a fast thinker. He pointed to Rags as an example of the yellow-dog breed. The terrier barked louder.

"Atta boy, doggie," a big sergeant in the crowd shouted. "You tell him where he gets off."

Rags was doing just that. He pranced excitedly in front of the spellbinder, his fuzzy coat vibrating, and barked with all the energy he could muster.

"As I was saying," the radical began, "why should you—?"

"Grup! Grup! Grup-erup-erup!" barked Rags.

"Go to it, puppy," a big soldier called. "You've got him out-talked!"

"Get that blasted mutt out o' here," the speaker shouted.

One of the radicals directed a vicious kick at Rags, and accompanied it with a raucous string of profanity. The kick didn't land. A fresh-faced training-camp student stepped in and blocked it, at the same time pushing the communist backward.

"Leave that dog alone," he ordered. "That's Rags, the First Division's old mascot. He don't rate kicks from you—or anybody!"

The Red flung an obscene epithet at the youngster and swung a gnarled fist. The lad blocked it with a boxer's skill and drove a clean, hard uppercut to the chin. The man went down.

His companions rushed the student. One of slipped a blackjack from his pocket and manoeuvred for a blow at the youngster's head, before anyone in the crowd realized what was afoot—that is, anyone except Rags. The dog had seen blackjacks in the hands of military police. He knew their use.

As the Red shifted to get a free swing, Rags wriggled himself into the clear space around the fighters. With a throaty growl the terrier left the ground. A slash of his teeth forced the blackjack from the man's hand. Rags worried it to one side, edged it carefully into the gutter, and started looking for a new opening in the fray, which had become general as the crowd backed Rags's defender. Before he could get in again it was halted abruptly. Half a dozen policemen, nightsticks swinging, forced their way into the melee. With a few punches and taps of their clubs they rounded up the radicals.

Rags ran to the gutter, seized the blackjack, and carried it to the sergeant in command of the police. The policeman snatched the weapon, glanced at it, and began a rapid-fire questioning of his prisoners. All denied ownership. Rags, who had been standing at a stiff point, burst into a fury of barking at the man from whom he had taken the blackjack.

The police sergeant grabbed the fellow.

"Look at his right wrist," a bystander shouted. "The pup took the thing away from him."

The police sergeant looked. Teeth marks were plainly visible. The prisoner wriggled and twisted, resisting arrest. The police sergeant swung a mighty Irish fist. There was no more resistance. Rags, hopping around excitedly, barked "three rousing cheers." The disturbers were loaded into a patrol wagon. Rags stood expectantly at the step. Nobody invited him to ride. So he trotted along behind the patrol wagon, paced on the sidewalk by the students who had seen the trouble. At the police station the terrier gave tongue as each prisoner was led out. When the last one was being herded inside, Rags almost got under the feet of the policeman who was guarding him.

"Take it easy, doggie," the patrolman advised. "You'll get plenty of chance to testify against these birds."

Rags paid no attention, but nosed his way in, pausing, as he slipped through the door, to give a disapproving jerk at the trousers of the rear-rank prisoner. Inside, he found them lined up in front of the sergeant. He went from one to another, barking. The feet of one or two moved restlessly. The policemen guarding these muttered, just so the prisoner could hear it:

"Take a kick at the dog, why don't you? I'm just hopin' that you do."

Nobody tried to kick Rags. But the racket he was making got on the nerves of the desk sergeant.

"Put that confounded pup out, one o' you!" he ordered.

"Sorry, sergeant," spoke up the boss of the arresting crew, "but that little pooch is our principal witness. He's that First Division mascot dog."

"Oh," said the desk sergeant. "Tell him to shut up for a minute, then, will you?"

One of the training-camp students, who had eased his way in, stepped forward and crouched beside Rags.

"Keep quiet, will you?" he said. "The sergeant wants to talk. Be still now."

Rags ceased barking, edged into a corner, stretched himself out, and went to sleep. The police finished their routine—photographing, fingerprinting and like. They discovered they had two prisoners, wanted elsewhere, for whom fat rewards were offered. One of them was the man Rags had disarmed.

"Say," spoke up the sergeant who had headed the arresting detail, "that pup was pretty smart. We ought to do something for him."

The chief came in. He listened to the story, noticed Rags asleep in the corner, and remarked:

"He's probably hungry. Hey, Bill!"

The station-house janitor came on a run.

"Were you callin', Chief?" he inquired.

"Yeah! Beat it over to the lunch-wagon an' get a couple o' lamb chops—tell Tony you want his best an' some bread with a lot o' gravy on it."

Bill hurried across the street. He returned, bearing a couple of grilled lamb chops and gravy-soaked bread. The chief shoved the food under Rags's nose.

"Wake up!" he shouted.

Rags obliged. He sniffed, wagged his tail, and fell to. He trimmed the chops to the bone and then disappointed the police.

"I want to see him try to bury those bones around here," a policeman remarked.

The point was that within a dozen blocks of the station house there was no vacant spot that was not paved. The terrier brushed the bones to one side and ate the bread. Then he resumed his nap. He wasn't interested in burying bones. He never had found it necessary.

Rags was yawning himself awake when the station house cat—all police stations seem to have cats—came strolling in. The cat, a big Persian Tom, saw the terrier, hissed and spat. Rags made a flying tackle, but when he landed the cat was on the sergeant's desk, The terrier dropped back to the door to get a running start. When he struck the desk the cat had taken refuge in the sergeant's lap. It had tried his cap first, and there were claw marks on the policeman's face to show where it had slipped downward. The sergeant hurried from behind the desk and carried the cat to a place of safety. Then he scolded Rags. It was not a friendly scolding. The scratches left by the cat in its frantic flight from Rags had stirred the policeman's temper. The terrier listened, standing at stiff point, until the sergeant ended his tirade with:

"An" if you wasn't an' army dog I'd kick you out o' here this minute."

Rags focused his good eye on the speaker, stood motionless for another half-minute, then faced about and stalked out of the police station. He never visited it again, although more than one cop tried to coax him in. His attitude was, as plainly as if expressed in words, "If you get so hot and bothered about my chasing a cat, stick to the cat."

As the summer wore on Rags began to display signs of boredom. He spent a great deal of time dozing by the lake. Now and then he was observed down by the shore, watching the minnows in the clear water. Several times residents of the camp tried to set him diving after them. Such urging was his cue to go elsewhere. The Plattsburg folk didn't know of his fishing in France, or they would have realized the terrier hadn't forgotten his adventure with the eel. In the end he stayed away from the lake altogether, and moved about only when he went with the family. It was not until he noticed the signs he had learned meant a move that he began to display real zest about the business of living.

When satisfied, beyond doubt, that the family was quitting Plattsburg, he started out on his round of farewells. At first he undertook to be a luncheon guest at each of the messes. Quickly realizing there wasn't time for this, he made the rounds rapidly, dropping in on all his friends, much after the manner of a departing officer leaving his p. p. c. (pour prendre conge) cards. He would remain a few moments and then pass onto the next place. He completed his visits barely in time to avoid delaying the departure of the family.

There were a few whom Rags missed. Some of these managed to be on hand to bid him a farewell as the automobile, taking the family and Rags to the train, pulled out of the army reservation. Others were at the railroad station. They shouted and waved their farewells as the train pulled out. Rags barked his reply from the baggage-car door. Separation from his family on trains didn't disturb him any more. He knew by experience that the major, or at least some one of them, would be waiting for him at the end of the journey. He settled down comfortably for the ride over the history-rich trail that once had been the military road from New York to Canada. Baggage-cars are not ideal for observation purposes. So Rags saw little of the shore of Lake Champlain, of storied Fort Edward, or of the glamorous Hudson Valley. His interest lay only in the finish of the journey, when he would rejoin the family again.

The train-ride ended in the Grand Central Terminal in New York. There Rags detrained into a bustle the like of which he had not seen since war days. Great throngs were rushing this way and that. The terrier kept on the jump to avoid being stepped on, even though the major guided him with a leash. There was a slow taxicab ride. The cab would travel a few blocks and then stop for several minutes, in a great crush of other vehicles. Again it would move for a short space only to halt once more. As the crush of traffic jerked along in this fashion, by fits and starts, Rags excitedly looked out first one window, then another of the cab. He was saying, as plainly as a dog could:

"I've seen crushes like this before, but where are the troops and the cannonade?"

The terrier was quiet, in a puzzled sort of way, when the taxicab finally drove on the government ferryboat, General Humphreys, at the Battery. He remained so as the craft moved out of its slip and across the harbor. When it pushed into dock at Governors Island with a great thudding and bumping, Rags came to life with a loud barking, as if asking what it was all about. The major stroked his neck and reassured him, but when the cab shot up the incline and swung up the drive toward the officers' quarters Rags renewed his barking. As he peered out of the cab he saw soldiers. Each of them wore on his shoulder the insignia of the First Division. The terrier was back with his old outfit.

CHAPTER THIRTEEN
THE OLD GANG AGAIN

FOR the first few days after his arrival at Governors Island, Rags was just another dog to many of the soldiers. Upstanding youngsters they were, friendly enough, but ignorant of the terrier's past. Most of them had been schoolboys in the white-hot days of the division's glory. The great mass of the soldiers of Soissions, St.-Mihiel and the Meuse-Argonne had gone back to civilian pursuits. To the youths who formed the peace skeleton of the once mighty unit the battles were only names, the victories tradition. But they cherished the names, and they strove earnestly to live up to the high tradition, wearing the fourragers—the green and gilt cord which recalled that the whole division had been cited for gallantry—with a high sense of pride. There was a leaven of old-timers, men who were veteran soldiers when the division was born, whose blouses scarce had space for their campaign ribbons and decorations. But nearly all of these were non-commissioned officers whose duties kept them in their offices. Rags did not meet them until he hunted them out.

True to his exploring habits, the terrier found them. At first they commented on his resemblance to the "pup that soldiered with Donovan." Then, remarking the blind eye, the crippled ear, the occasional limp and cough, they read the name on his collar—"First Division Rags." They made bold to question the major. His identity verified, Rags became, so far as the old-timers were concerned, the living symbol of the division's valor. As soon as the younger soldiers learned the story, their devotion to the terrier became as deep as, and less restrained than, that of the veterans. These latter knew Rags had no use for cuddling. They never offered it. But the younger men sought to pet the terrier, lapdog fashion, and were snubbed for their pains. When such attentions were offered, Rags would straighten his tail and march away with the outraged dignity of a general. Little by little Rags got his viewpoint accepted. Only new recruits offended. The terrier resumed his old pastime of lunching and dining at such messes as took his fancy; or of dropping in after meals for a snack. He was busy exploring, what with stables, numerous barracks, boats coming and going, and the prison at Castle Williams; so he often turned up at odd times seeking food.

This habit sometimes made difficulty for new recruits who were doing a turn at cook's police. Lately arrived at the island, they did not know Rags. His demands for food annoyed them—kitchen police are seldom in an affable mood—and now and then got rough with him. They seldom repeated the offence. Usually some older soldier enlightened them, and Rags never appeared to bear them any grudge. The terrier even forgave Private Jones, who in a fit of pique hurled a potato at him. Rags, standing just inside the door, dodged the potato. It smacked against the highly polished shoes of Sergeant Wymms, who was coming in.

"What's the idea of the horseplay, you spud manicures?" Wymms demanded.

The sergeant wasn't especially angry, just stern, as usual, for discipline's sake. He was mollified when Jones seized a rag and cleaned the potato from his footgear.

"I wasn't throwin' at you, Sergeant," Jones explained. "I was heavin' at that darned pooch."

"You were what?"

"Chasin' the pooch—the little yellow mutt in the corner!"

Wymms glanced at Rags. The terrier wigwagged a greeting and barked a friendly "howdy." Wymms stiffened and faced Jones.

"You threw a spud at Rags!" he roared. "Why you—"

The sergeant's wrath choked off the words. A second later his fist crashed against Jones's jaw. The man staggered backward, stumbled and fell. Wymms stood waiting for him to get up. The sergeant was thoroughly angry. The four rows of ribbons on his breast heaved up and down as he struggled to control himself. It didn't occur to him that poor Jones hadn't the slightest idea of Rags's identity or history. He set himself for another punch. Then Rags interfered. He had been standing motionless, at point, from the moment the sergeant had entered. Now he hopped between Wymms and the fallen Jones, and sat back on his haunches, with paws uplifted, saying as plainly as he could: "He didn't mean any harm. Don't hit him again."

Wymms stepped back in amazement. Jones, struggling to his feet, looked at the little terrier in surprise. Rags held his position and thumped the floor with his tail.

"All right, Rags: have it your way," the sergeant told him. Then to Jones: "You can thank the dog I'm not trimmin' you right. An' you'd better find out about him before you toss any more spuds at him!"

Rags followed Wymms out of the door. He hurried down to H Company mess, where everybody knew him, while Private Jones nursed his sore jaw and made inquiries about Rags. Jones appreciated the intervention and, in cultivating a friendship, discovered one of the things that annoyed the terrier. At Sheridan, Plattsburg, Benning, and other camps Rags had been able to quench his thirst in a lake or reasonably pure stream. He drank when thirsty, without bothering anyone. There was plenty of water around the island, but it wasn't drinkable. One sniff told Rags that. So he sometimes was thirsty for hours, not having learned to make his need for water known. Donovan, when they were not near a stream, had always supplied him without being asked. Jones, trailing the dog around to make friends, noticed this, and explained the situation to several old-timers. Soon every company provided a pan which was kept filled for Rags. The terrier understood about them after he had been introduced to them once.

Rags's distaste for cats threatened his popularity with the womenfolk on the post, at first. Soon they found that the terrier did the cats no harm. He never stalked them, always gave them a fair start, and went his way as soon as he had chased them up a tree. The exercise did the cats good. They were getting fat and lazy in the easy, well-fed life of the garrison. With the other dogs on the post Rags made friends. His especial cronies were two splendid collies, who, much to their annoyance, were always kept beautifully groomed by their mistress, the wife of an officer. Rags folk respected his prejudices against bathtubs as much as they could. He was asked to endure only an occasional flea-dipping. They didn't brush and comb him, nor did they tie any ribbons on him.

Perhaps this was why the collies regarded him with a sort of awe—seemed to be asking him, "How do you get away with it."

The collies, despite their grooming, were provident dogs. They saved their bones and carefully buried them in a corner of the parade-ground. Rags developed the habit of saving his left-over bones and delivering them to the collies. He sat and watched while his friends thriftily hid them away. Nobody ever saw Rags do any digging, himself. Long ago, in France, he had learned that burying bones was a futile labor; in a few hours a dog might be miles away from the hiding-place. But the collies accepted his offerings with gusto, so Rags continued to bring them.

Rags, comparatively speaking, was an old resident of the island when the chow arrived. It was an ill-tempered beast, and at first sight took a violent dislike to Rags. It was on leash at the time, so Rags ignored the hostile outburst and went about his business—but with deliberation that indicated he was in no wise afraid. The terrier merely followed his custom of hunting no trouble. The chow misread him and snarled more viciously. It happened that the chow's owner was quartered in a house Rags had visited frequently when another officer lived there. Rags now avoided it, but continued his calls at the houses on either side. The chow, often tied up in the back yard or chained to the front porch, barked and snarled viciously whenever Rags appeared. The terrier paid no attention. Rags would no more quarrel with a chained dog than with a statue. But it was inevitable that the chow would not always be kept chained. Those who have no more sense than to own vicious dogs—few dogs are really vicious—can't be expected to have sense keep them always tied up.

The chow, on the loose and exploring, sighted Rags sunning himself near the ferry landing. He made a bee line for the terrier, snapping and snarling. Before he could pounce, Rags was on his feet and met the attack with a slashing grab for the chow's nose. Rags instinctively knew that there was no use trying for a hold on that heavily protected throat. The chow paused with a snarl. Rags fought silently, damaging his enemy's nose considerably, but unable to get a hold he could keep. The chow was fast and clever, much faster than the police dog Rags had fought at Benning. He fastened a mean hold on Rags's war-torn ear, the same one the police dog had worked on. But realizing that was getting him nowhere, he let go and slashed at the terrier's throat. Rags dodged and jabbed the nose again.

Meanwhile the soldiers on duty at the dock were trying to decide what to do. The battlers moved so fast that the men were afraid to strike at the chow, lest they injure Rags.

A veteran sergeant, passing on other duty, snatched a club from one of the military police and was maneuvering for a blow at the chow when a couple of white-and-gold thunderbolts almost knocked him over as they hurled themselves into the fray—Rags's collie friends. They made no mistake as to which fighter they were grabbing. The chow's neck armor was not quite impervious to their long fangs. Its spine was at the mercy of their powerful jaws. So far as the collies were concerned, Fort Jay was due to lose a bad canine citizen without much delay. But the chow was no fool. He twisted, slashed and charged his way out of the melee, and ran for his quarters and safety. Rags lay down, panting, with the collies solicitously on either side of him, one licking his torn ear.

It was a most unorthodox ending to a dog fight. But the more the soldiers analyzed it, the more their respect for Rags's courage grew. The terrier might have run to any of the groups around the dock for protection. It would have been given. The chow was twice his size, and his age and war record would have kept his prestige. But the soldiers almost worshiped the courage that had made Rags face his enemy and fight it out without giving an inch of ground. The duel established Rags, long regarded as a sort of animated legend, as a real personage in his own right.

More and more the men of the Sixteenth Infantry, which was the only unit of the First Division on the island, began to take a proprietary pride in Rags. Recognizing the major and his family as the duly authorized custodians—Rags's family never made any other claim—and Rags as the division mascot, they adopted the theory that the terrier was particularly attached to the Sixteenth. The men of H Company undertook to convince the rest of the regiment that Rags really was a member of that outfit. They pointed out that hardly a day passed without the terrier's visiting the mess at H, whereas he dropped in on the other units at odd times only.

Rags recognized the symptoms. He began distributing his patronage impartially over the entire garrison. Also he displayed a new interest in the men who appeared almost daily at the island, in a small launch from somewhere down the bay. These soldiers and officers wore the shoulder shield of the First Division, but the regimental insignia of the Eighteenth Infantry. They came from Fort Hamilton, where division headquarters was located, to make their reports to the corps area commander. Old soldiers, they knew all about Rags and were at pains to greet him cordially. They felt elated that the terrier should an interest in their comings and goings. For several days he met them on their arrival and saw them off on their departure. Then, one evening, he surprised them by hopping into the launch. A sergeant was about to set him back on the dock when the Senior officer intervened.

"Rags wants to visit us at Hamilton," the officer observed. "If he does he can. Let him alone."

"Very good, sir. But if the major doesn't mind, I was thinking the children will be worrying about him."

"Right. I'd forgotten. I'll call up Rags's folks and tell 'em he's visiting us, and that we didn't kidnap him."

In such fashion Rags made his first visit to Fort Hamilton; had his first glimpse of the peace-time head-quarters of the First Division. There were men in the Eighteenth who had known him in France; more than that, there were men in the headquarters detail who had known Donovan. They made him welcome, doubly welcome, because they felt Rags's action had "taken them Sixteenth Infantry lobsters down a peg."

"Good ol' Rags," an elderly beribboned sergeant told the terrier as he scratched his back, "you wouldn't let those stuffed uniforms over on the island high-hat us, would you?"

"Course he wouldn't," cut in another veteran. "He knows those birds think they're the whole division just because they're over at corps. Maybe when they know Rags came over here they'll remember the Eighteenth's part of the First, too."

Rags thumped his tail in approval, made the rounds of the companies, and finally settled on headquarters company's mess for his dinner. Some choice bits of the lamb stew were set aside for him. He was, in the eyes of the soldiers—and officers too—a most desirable and distinguished guest.

Meantime Rags's folks had been informed he'd gone visiting. The officer who delivered the message had some qualms lest the terrier's absence make the children unhappy. It didn't. The youngsters had perfect confidence in the dog's devotion to them. Sue, in fact, appeared able to read Rags's mind.

"Those soldiers in H Company," she said, "have been thinking they owned Rags. They've been trying to get him away from us. He's just gone away to show them. Now maybe they'll stop it."

Her guess proved correct. Rags remained at Hamilton for two days, got acquainted with everybody including half a dozen friendly dogs, chased a few cats, sampled all the cooking, and on the third day was waiting at the dock for the boat. The moment it touched the dock he hurried up to the Hardenbergh house and sought out the children announcing with bark and tail-wave: "Well, I'm back, and I hope you're glad to see me." They were and told him so. Soldiers of the Sixteenth also were glad, although a bit crestfallen. For two days the men of the Eighteenth had been dinning into them the news that Rags had settled the question of his status. No regiment could claim him—much less any company. He was a division dog. And that was that.

CHAPTER FOURTEEN
THE SIDEWALKS OF NEW YORK

R AGS'S trip to Hamilton apparently gave him a zest for voyaging.
Since the day he had landed on the island from the ferry, he never
had shown any inclination to board the craft again. A few days after the
Hamilton adventure he trotted down to the ferry dock and started
aboard. The military police, and the men in charge of the ferry, were all
for keeping him off. Regulations barred dogs not on leash. But the chief
of staff himself came striding down to the gang-plank and curtly told
them that, if Rags wanted a boat ride, the regulations did not apply. Rags
inspected the boat from bow to stern and, when it bumped into its slip,
ran off at the heels of the soldier who carried the mail.

In the street the terrier had a bad time of it. The crush of traffic
bewildered him. After several narrow escapes from automobiles he got
across to Battery Park and caught up with the mail-carrier who had not
noticed him. As the man started across the lower end of Broadway
toward Whitehall, taxis, autos, and trucks were dashing in every direction.
It was too hectic for Rags. He hated automobiles. The soldier was a
dozen paces into the street when Rags set up a great barking. The man
looked around, grinned, then returned and picked Rags up under his arm.
Together they went to the Army Building at 39 Whitehall, where
recruiting, information, and certain other army administrative matters are
handled.

As the soldier delivered the mail to the various offices, and gathered
up the messages to be taken back to Governors Island, Rags made a
survey of the building. There is always a horsy smell about the place—
the odor of saddle soap and harness leather. Rags seemed to be looking
for the horses. Instead, he found several veterans—officers and
noncoms—tucked away in odd corners of the rambling old building.
These recognized him and made him welcome, although surprised and
somewhat puzzled as to the manner of his getting there. An old
recruiting sergeant took him up to the Army Information Service, and
introduced him to the snappy young officer in charge.

"I've heard about him," the officer admitted. "What's all this about
his being wounded and gassed?"

The sergeant, who had known both Donovan and Rags in France,
went into details. When he had concluded the officer arose and gravely
saluted the terrier. His surprise was acute when Rags returned the

compliment with his own canine adaptation of the military gesture. He grasped Rags's saluting paw and shook it warmly. Rags thumped the floor with his tail and gave an appreciative bark. The officer reached for a pad, picked up a pencil, and turned to the sergeant.

"Let's get the dope all down in proper order," he suggested.

The sergeant went over the story again. When the officer had finished making notes he turned to the terrier.

"Rags," he announced, "you are elected to become famous here and now."

The word "famous" wasn't in Rags's vocabulary. But from the tone and the attitude of the uniformed folk around him he took it for granted as something quite all right, and wigwagged a message of concurrence. The officer murmured an order to a soldier, and presently a man appeared with a big black box, set it up on legs, threw a dark cloth over it, and then stuck his head under the cloth. Rags never had seen a camera before and he watched the proceedings with breathless interest. The officer lifted Rags from the floor and set him on top of a desk. Rags focused his good eye on the lens of the camera, which, from his position in front of it, somewhat resembled the muzzle of a one-pounder. He looked inquiringly at the officer as the photographer began sprinkling powder into his flash-gun. The terrier's keen nose caught the scent of that powder. He hopped off the desk and flattened himself on the floor, just as he had learned to do when he heard the rattle of shell coming his way in the old war days. The officer was puzzled, but the sergeant read Rags's mind.

"He's caught a whiff of the powder, sir," he explained. "I don't suppose he's ever had a picture taken, an' he prob'ly thinks the camera is some kind of gun."

"That's right. He would smell the stuff. But we've got to get his picture and we can't take it here without a flash."

"If we all sit on the desk with him, he'll soon understand that it's all right."

So they placed the terrier back on the desk and sat on either side of him.

"Just fire the flash," the officer ordered. "No need of wasting plates. We want the dog alone, when we can get him."

The photographer raised his flash-gun and pressed the trigger. In the stillness of the room the click of the release was ever so slight, but in the fraction of a second before the hammer struck the firing-cap Rags was on the floor again, hugging it as closely as ever he had hugged the ground in France. The men laughed. Rags got up a bit sheepishly and cocked his eye at them reproachfully. He took a few steps toward the door, hesitated, then came back and sat down. Wisps of smoke drifting down from the pall which the flash had left near the ceiling made him cough. But he stayed.

The men then decided to let Rags watch the flash from the photographer's end while they took turns sitting on the desk. After the first smoke was cleared out the officer took his turn. Then the sergeant was shot. Rags sat motionless and watched. When the smoke again cleared, he moved gingerly toward the desk, looked back at the camera, and then, without waiting to be asked, hopped up on the desk and faced the lens. The sergeant dropped his cap on Rags's head, and as the terrier shook the headgear down over one ear the photographer fired his flash and made the picture. Rags barked, shook off the cap, and pounded the desk with his tail. Then he waited expectantly.

"Go ahead, shoot another," the officer ordered. "Make it snappy before the smoke comes down."

The photographer obeyed. Rags again applauded. But still he sat on the desk.

"Holy smoke!" laughed the officer. "The little cuss is just like a human—one taste of the camera and you can't get him away from it."

Then the smoke began to drift downward. It made Rags cough violently and brought tears to his good eye. So they opened the windows and carried him into the corridor until the room was cleared.

The smoke gone, they brought Rags back and took another picture. This done, the photographer folded up his camera and departed. Rags gazed after him regretfully.

"Don't look so down-hearted," the officer advised him. "I'll bet you a T-bone against one of your fleas I'll get your picture in every paper in town."

When the time came for Rags to return to the island, it developed that the mail-carrier had departed. But the officer had no intention of risking Rags's life and limb in the mad traffic of the Battery. He summoned a soldier.

"Take him over to the island," he ordered. "Carry him if he'll let you. And don't let anything happen to him."

The soldier moved to pick up Rags. The terrier edged away.

"He probably won't be carried," the officer commented. "But keep close to him, watch him every second."

The soldier started for the door, calling to Rags to follow. The terrier hesitated, then, apparently deciding that he was being invited to dinner, obeyed. He was getting hungry. Down the stairs they went and out into Whitehall Street. The soldier started across the street. Rags eyed the automobiles dashing past, halted on the curb, and barked. The soldier returned.

"Come on," he said. "I'm lookin' out for you."

Rags merely sat down and stared up at him. The soldier reached to pick him up. Rags this time made no objection, but once across the street he wriggled to be set down again. The soldier finally got the idea. Where automobiles were menacing, Rags preferred be carried. At all other times he wanted to travel under his own power. At the ferry the soldier found there was no need for him to escort Rags farther. The military police and the men on the boat had been watching for him since the mail-carrier returned without him. Rags trotted down the gangplank, and when he reached the deck turned to see if his escort was following. The soldier waved a farewell.

"So long old-timer," he cried. "See you again time."

Rags mistook the wave for a salute, and returned it with his usual punctiliousness. Then he turned and loped up the stairs to the officers' deck.

"Well, I'll be doggoned!" the soldier muttered as he strode out of the ferry building. The M. P.'s laughed at him. Rags's saluting was an old story to the soldiers stationed on the island. When their amusement had subsided, however, they gave serious consideration to Rags's visit to New York. Suppose, they reasoned, the terrier should come over some day and find no one to take care of him in the traffic! He might be injured or killed. Then, again, some one might steal him. They decided to make an informal report and point out the dangers. They did.

A few days later, when Rags felt the call of the great city, he found himself barred from the ferry-boat. The order had gone out that, unless escorted, he was not to visit New York. Rags pleaded and coaxed through two ferry-boat trips, and then dejectedly went away. He hurried down to where the boat from Fort Hamilton usually tied up, but it was not there. He moved to another dock and inspected closely a boat he had often noticed but to which he had paid little close attention before. It was an army mine-planter that maintained communication between Fort Jay, at Governors Island, and Fort Hancock, down at Sandy Hook. With the air of one who is determined to go a-voyaging somewhere, he scrambled aboard. One of the soldiers sought to put him off. An officer intervened.

"Let him alone," he ordered. "Go ashore and send word that Rags is visiting the First Engineers, down at Hancock."

It is a rather long trip to Sandy Hook, and after the first hour of travel Rags displayed a nervous restlessness. It was plain this was a more extended voyage than he had purposed. The colonel who had permitted him aboard reassured him—told him he'd meet some old friends. He did. Engineering outfits in the army hang together more consistently than either infantry, artillery, or cavalry. The men, especially the non-coms, reenlist from term to term and grow old in the service. The officers usually stick with the same unit until they are advanced to the higher grades. All in all, they are a little more compact than other branches of the service. So, when Rags arrived at Hancock, he ran into a regular old-home party. On all sides were men he had run across in the old days. There were, of course, many strange faces, but the old-timers were far more numerous than anywhere else he had been. They wore their First Division insignia with the air of men who had helped create its glory. Rags was no legend to them; he was as closely linked to their lives as the battle scars on their bodies.

They held a party for him at the post exchange. The choicest tidbits of the various messes were gathered and spread out for his approval and consumption. When the hour for "taps" approached, a bed was made for him in the guardhouse, out of a couple of pillows covered with a blanket. He declined to turn in as early as his friends suggested, so they allowed him to have his way and explore the post. It was nearing dawn when he finally drifted into the guardhouse, stretched himself out on the pillows, and went to sleep. Soldiers lounging around the guardroom noticed that he awakened with a start at the first blast of a big coast-defense gun. They saw him run to the door, cock his good ear upward, and listen intently. Another gun boomed. The annual target practice was on and the guns began firing as soon as it was light enough to see. They would continue to fire through the day, until haze or fog obscured the targets.

At the second discharge Rags stood, in uncertain fashion, on the threshold. He was still listening. When the third discharge crashed out Rags looked inquiringly from one soldier to another.

"Thought he was a war dog," a young recruit piped up. "He don't seem to know what that firin's all about."

"You poor sap," a corporal growled, "he's listenin' for the return message."

"What return message?"

"Listen, greenhorn. When Rags first heard guns there was always a

86

comeback. Our side fired, and pretty soon the other fellow sent us a receipt—in the form of a lot o' shell. You could hear 'em comin', and you hit the grit. Rags is listenin' for a shell."

"Oh!"

The corporal turned to Rags:

"Come on, old-timer; let's beat it out o' here and I'll show you how the big babies work."

The dog followed the corporal down to the emplacements where the big guns rose out of their pits, hurled their ton of destruction, and dropped back again, as if exhausted by the effort. Rags watched for a time, frequently glancing at the corporal in puzzled fashion. It was plain he was wondering why the other side didn't shoot back. In the end he lost interest and went over to the post exchange. His attitude indicated he intended to stay awhile at Hancock, which pleased the engineers mightily.

Once again, however, Rags's personal preferences were overruled. From Fort Jay came a request that that he be sent home forthwith. At first the engineers didn't understand why the terrier's visit to them should be cut short. The New York morning newspapers seldom reached Hancock before afternoon. When they arrived the business was explained. From almost every one of them peered a likeness of Rags, and under the picture was a brief summary of his war record. The army information officer had told the world about the terrier. Without further ado Rags was coaxed aboard the mine-planter and started back for Governors Island. There he found the folks somewhat indignant over his absence. A great many reporters and camera men had been around to interview him. They had been disappointed at not finding him at home. It was too late, when he finally arrived, to make any pictures. What was his idea in always being gadding, anyhow?

Rags paid no attention to the recriminations. He was hungry and hurried up to see the folks and get a snack. This business attended to, he returned to the dock. It was his intention, evidently, to go back to Hancock. But the mine-planter was gone. Rags turned away with the air of a dog who feels he has been abused. He ambled slowly toward the stables. The sergeant there was always sympathetic. But he had gone to town on pass. So Rags went home and curled up in his quarters in the living-room. His air of dejection worried the family at first, but finally his devotion to the children overcame his disappointment and he became his usual cheerful self.

Next morning, before Rags had a chance to get off the island, a delegation of soldiers took him in hand and introduced him to a gathering of a dozen or so men armed with the black boxes Rags had first seen on his New York visit. As soon as he saw them he sat down and set himself for the flash and bang. But none came. They had him shake hands with the general. Still he waited in vain for the flash. They placed him on a gun. Still no flash. He cocked his good eye at them in reproach, as if to say: "If you're going to shoot that thing, shoot it; I'm not afraid of it." Then they sat him on a big cannon-ball—a Civil War relic. Here he almost grinned, as if to say: "Ah, now you'll fire that thing." Again, of course, there being plenty of daylight, there was no flash. So, with an air of disgust, Rags left them. They followed and found him in the stable sergeant's office, eating a belated breakfast. Once again they set up their cameras. This time they got their flashlight apparatus out. Rags looked at them in a bored fashion and went on eating. When the flash was fired his interest revived. But no matter what they did, they couldn't get another picture of him eating. He insisted on sitting and facing the camera.

CHAPTER FIFTEEN
THE PRICE OF PROMINENCE

NOT long after his intensive photographic adventure, Rags discovered what must have seemed to him a post-wide conspiracy against his comfort. The newspaper stories about him brought many dog-lovers to the island to see him. Some were the type who talked baby talk to him, who knelt down and tried to kiss and cuddle him, a performance which always caused him to depart without ceremony. After a time the appearance of a stranger in civilian dress was Rags's cue to streak it from the stables. By keeping an eye on the ferry landing he was able to get out of sight before unwelcome admirers could get close enough to interfere with him.

Eventually his hide-out at the stables was discovered, and when inquiries were made for him some of the soldiers would dig him out and proudly put him on parade. So he changed his practice and, when suspicious dog-lovers appeared, sought the sanctuary of his own fireside. The children, he soon found, would always protect him. Regardless of the prominence of the seeker after Rags, unless the children knew the terrier would be glad to see the person, it was just too bad—but Rags wasn't to be found. Life became the pleasant old routine again. But soon Rags's friends found a new cross for him to bear.

Some one had planted in the minds of the soldiers the idea that Rags should be entered in a Brooklyn dog show. They carried the proposal to the major, who declined to have anything to do with it, but explained that he did not feel authorized to veto it, if the men of the division favored it. He suggested, though, that he didn't believe Rags would be keen for it. The soldiers had their hearts set on the plan. Little encouragement came from the officers, who explained that although they regarded Rags as the outstanding dog of the century, they couldn't testify as to his ancestry. In vain they explained that at dog shows it was not the personal accomplishments of an individual dog that counted, but his conformance to certain specifications held by experts to indicate perfection of type. Show dogs, they explained, were supposed to have long lines of pure-bred ancestors, and nobody contended Rags was a pure-bred. He was just a shaggy little terrier, undoubtedly partly Irish, but with a goodly sprinkling of various kinds of Scotch—a mixture incidentally, that seems to run strongly to warriors. But no one in authority forbade the men to enter Rags, so they went ahead with their plans.

The womenfolk of the garrison were greatly taken with the idea—that is, those outside of Rags's own family. Their first thought, of course, was to doll up the terrier. When the opening assault was made on his comfort he was so amazed that he didn't even resist until the ordeal was nearly ended. The wife of a warrant officer coaxed him into her kitchen, and with the aid of a couple of neighbors scrubbed and polished Rags as he never had been scrubbed before in all his life. Then, while a couple of women held him, she combed and brushed him until his coat fairly glistened. To complete the job she tied a bow of ribbon to his collar, and after surveying him with a glow of pride in her work, permitted him to go his way.

"It's a little early to start cleaning him up," she explained, "But if we keep right at it he'll be used to it by the time the show comes off, and we can send him up looking elegant."

Rags, outside the house, stood in a sort of daze, as if he were saying to himself—like the old woman in the nursery jingle—"Can this be I?" Seemingly he decided it was, and wasted no more time in meditation. He headed for the stables, pausing now and then, trying to paw the ribbon off. Failing, he detoured slightly to a big puddle on the edge of the corral. There he rolled with gusto, until he was thoroughly muddied and the ribbon was limp as a piece of wilted lettuce. This done, he sought out the stable sergeant and sat up, pawing pleadingly for the ribbon to be removed. The sergeant obliged.

"Who," he demanded, "has been tying these sissified decorations on Rags? He's a war dog, not a confounded lapdog!"

Rags thanked the sergeant with tail-thump and bark, went outside, and gave himself a satisfied shake. He stood for a moment in a meditative pose and then dashed toward the Fort Hamilton boat-landing. Not finding the boat, he retraced his steps and made a wide circle of the reservation to give his coat time to dry. The family scolded when he came in dripping with mud. In his promenade he almost ran into the woman who had given him his earlier polishing. She saw him and could hardly believe her eyes.

"Why," she cried, "he's all dirty again!" and made a grab for him. Rags did a quick side-step and made his best speed down the roadway, easily eluding a couple of little girls who tried to head him off. Several small boys, seeing the chase, undertook to overhaul Rags. The terrier cut around to a row of officers' quarters and took refuge in the home of a lieutenant. The lieutenant's wife welcomed him—and gave him another scrubbing. Dejectedly he took his leave. Stealthily he sought his puddle, rolled in a few times, shook himself, and hid in the stables until he was dry enough to go home. He approached the major's quarters with some misgivings. After his experience of two scrubbings in one day, anything might happen. But beyond a dry brushing to get the mud off his coat he was unmolested. He didn't mind dry brushings—he rather liked them. They had a pleasant scratchy feeling. For that matter, he had long ago become resigned to his flea-dip baths—when the family administered them. But for comparative strangers to scrub him with soap and water, getting some of the soap in his good eye, was nothing less than an outrage, from Rags's viewpoint. If the family knew what had befallen him, they gave no sign. The home was the same comforting easy-going place it always had been.

He ventured out next day warily. But the siren voice of women again trapped him. He acquired another suds bath and a new ribbon. Again he took his mud roll, induced the stable sergeant to rid him of the ribbon, and sought out the Fort Hamilton boat. This time it was at the landing and he went aboard without ceremony. The Fort Hamilton soldiery greeted him with cheers—its womenfolk welcomed him with scrub-brushes. The plan to enter him in the dog show was division-wide. There was nothing for it but to go back to the island. Rags took the first available boat, without even bothering to roll in a puddle. The soldiers on the boat complimented him on his spick-and-span appearance, but when they noticed the frantic efforts to rid himself of the ribbon, they obliged him and removed it.

Back at the island, he headed for home, ambling along in dejected fashion, tail drooping and head close to the ground. He didn't notice the warrant officer's wife who had initiated the bathtub persecutions until he was almost under her feet. He dodged instinctively but she made no move to molest him. Instead, she acted pleased and surprised.

"Why, Rags," she cried, "you look as pretty as a picture! Why don't you stay that way?"

Then she bent, patted him, and moved on. Soldiers told him the same thing. Even his friend the stable sergeant complimented him.

"You look all dressed up, old-timer," the sergeant informed him. "I didn't have any idea you were so handsome."

Not until the fourth day was Rags again subjected to the scrub-brush torture. Cannily he realized that the longer he could keep his well-groomed appearance the fewer baths would be inflicted on him. But the ribbons he refused to tolerate. His friends the collies solved that problem for him, so that he no longer had to bother the stable sergeant. Either of the collies could nose out the loose ends of the ribbon. A quick pull and the bow was undone. Another jerk and the thing was dragged loose from Rags's collar. Before the show date rolled around a compromise had been effected. Rags kept as clean as he could, and submitted to the baths with resignation. The women refrained from tying ribbons on him.

The day before the show opened was virtually a holiday on the island. Rags's entry had been sent in beforehand—they listed him as Irish terrier. The time had come to deliver him in person. An imposing delegation of bemedaled veterans was selected to accompany him. Washed and brushed until he fairly listened, Rags was transported to the show. There an entry-clerk looked him over superciliously and declined to accept him as Irish.

"Make it Scotch, then," the soldiers urged.

It appeared Rags didn't qualify as Scotch, either.

"Well, then, enter him as a war dog. He sure rates that."

Unfortunately, there was no such class. The clerk—and the officials who had been called in to settle the affair—regretted it, but there was no place in the show for Rags. A dejected group of soldier-men drove slowly to Governors Island. Their indignation knew no bounds. How did these dog-show people get that way, anyhow? If they didn't have a war-dog class, why didn't they? Hang it all! Rags had forgotten more than those stuffed dogskins that were getting ribbons would ever know. Furthermore, he could lick any and all of 'em. The soldiers of the First Division were mightily upset. And that wasn't all. The officers, and the rest of the army, would give them the horse laugh!

As it turned out, neither the officers nor the army did anything of the sort. The indignation against the barring of Rags became epidemic. Those who had, with good-natured tolerance, predicted that the dog-show people would not accept the entry of Rags, became the most outspoken protestants when their prediction came true. First Division veterans, who had gone back to civilian life after the Armistice, became hot and bothered about the matter and wrote letters to the newspapers. Editorial writers and columnists joined in the clamor. The old cry of "What Price Glory?" place to "What Breed Hero?" The only individual who seemed undisturbed was Rags himself. He was the center of a storm of controversy, but he was no longer the object of industrious scrub-brush experts. He found he could resume his old habits—make his old ports of call—without being haled into a bath at every turn. Rags found nothing to complain about.

Nevertheless, the terrier's friends pressed their campaign to vindicate

Rags's standing as the "world's champion dog." They delved into every detail of his heroic history and gave the information to the world. A newspaper printed an allegorical interview with him. Major-General Robert Lee Bullard, who had commanded the First Division with distinction, was photographed shaking hands with him. His picture got into the newspapers again and again. And on October 17, 1926, his claim to show-dog standing was vindicated. The Long Island Kennel Club invited the First Division to enter Rags, at the bench show in the Twenty-third Regiment Armory in Brooklyn. A special class had been created for him. The invitation was accepted. Rags again found himself the object of much dolling up by the womenfolk. But this time the soldiers voted with Rags. No extra scrubbing and no ribbons. The ladies, of course, persevered, as is their habit, but with the help of the soldiers Rags managed to evade them most of the time. His coat was a bit muddy when he took his place at the show in front of a big banner which told the story of his war exploits. There wasn't any competition, and Rags came away with the ribbon of the "War-dog sweepstakes championship."

The post had hardly settled down from celebration of the bench-show victory when the Junior League announced it would like Rags to attend its show for "Famous Pets of Famous People." The invitation was duly placed on file while the parade-ground lawyers argued about Rags's status. One group, composed largely of old-timers, contended that Rags was no pet. That he was famous they conceded, but as a "people and not a "pet." As Sergeant MacGregor put it: "The division is Rags's pet; Rags's isn't anybody's pet. He's a soldier dog, an' soldiers ain't pets."

The discussion delayed acceptance of the invitation, so the Junior League sent a committee around to see about it. The chairman of the delegation was a tall, lithe brunette—the horsy, outdoor type. Rags, after reconnoitering from a safe distance, trotted up and offered his friendship to her. She accepted, scratched his neck and head, and then turned to listen to MacGregor's apologies for the delay in answering the invitation.

"You see, it's like this, miss," he stammered. "Rags is getting old, and, like all old veterans, he likes his ease. When we send him to a show the women around here pester him most gosh-awfully with baths an' ribbons an' things."

"Yeah? Go on."

"Then, miss, you see there's some disagreement among us. 'Taint been decided yet that he's a pet. Some of the men insist he's a famous people."

"I see. Well, the famous people will be there with their pets. So if you want to send Rags as a famous person—or people, as you put it—its okay with us. You can bring your whole First Division along as his pet if you like. But we want Rags."

The girl's voice was a musical contralto. Rags cocked his good ear toward her and then sat up on his haunches, paws uplifted. He liked that voice. The sergeant noticed.

"Looks like Rags has settled it for himself," he told her. "He don't make friends with many folks that way."

"Oh, we'll get along. Will you send him over?"

"Yes, miss, we'll have him there."

"Thanks, old top. You're a good egg. Tell the ladies to lay off on the bathtub stuff. Rags doesn't like it. And it doesn't do him any special good."

She shook hands with the sergeant and turned to Rags.

"So long, little warrior," she purred, taking the up-lifted paw. "See you later."

The sergeant explained matters to the post personnel, and particularly to the feminine contingent thereof, as to the Junior League views on scrubbing terriers. So Rags attended the show with his entire collection of fleas, a matter which brought some complaint later from the owner of a handsome collie with which Rags became chummy. But then, the man had no real cause for complaint. The news-picture men concentrated on Rags, and paid little attention to the other dogs. The collie had almost as many pictures as Rags, because, after they got acquainted, the terrier refused to pose without him.

CHAPTER SIXTEEN
TELLING THE MARINES

WHILE Rags was resting on his laurels another famous war dog dined more heartily than an aging veteran should, and in a few days was buried with the honors of war—Sergeant-Major Jiggs, of the United States Marine Corps. Rags never had met him so naturally did not mourn him. But the marines decided it would be good policy for them to introduce the sergeant-major's successor to Rags. This dog, a fine English bull, presented to the corps by a famous athlete—an ex-marine—was named Jiggs II. Being a rookie, he had to start at the bottom as a private. With no war record behind him, he had scant prestige, and got none of the attention from the newspapers that had been accorded the veteran sergeant-major.

The marines decided a meeting with Rags might bring their mascot a bit of notice. They hoped the sleek, well-trained thoroughbred would outshine the army hero as thoroughly as their own natty uniforms out-styled the doughboys. The rivalry between the services has always has been keen. Marine Corps history has it that a great victory was won by a few marines with the help of the Deity. The army version is that the marines certainly were few, but that in their excitement they mistook certain crack regular-army regiments for Omnipotence. The rivalry goes on.

The army men greeted the proposal with glee. Rags, they reasoned, certainly would show up that leather-neck pup. What, they demanded, did a dog just out an English kennel know about military matters? Rags, on the other hand, "had everything."

"I'll bet you," a young corporal announced, "that Rags can outdrill him, outsmart him, outrun him, out-think him—an' then lick him!"

"You're right," Sergeant MacGregor concurred, "but Rags won't get a chance to lick him. Rags's fighting days are over!"

"Aw, have a heart, Sarge. Let's show up that gyrene bunch right. It'll be easy pickin's for Rags!"

"You heard me the first time. Rags ain't doin' no fightin'. He's too old."

"Well, if Rags starts it an' is winnin', can we let him go?"

"If he starts, we'll see. But I'll bust the first guy I catch settin' him on."

"I bet you he starts it. He don't like leathernecks no more'n we do."

Rags, it turned out, didn't care much for the snappily dressed marines. He turned up his nose at them. But he displayed no prejudice against Jiggs II. With tail swaying a friendly greeting, he trotted up to the great-chested bull and nosed him in pleasant fashion. Jiggs returned the greeting and the two stood with muzzles together, for all the world like a couple of cronies whispering comments on the rest of the company. A rookie soldier, who had not heard of MacGregor's ultimatum, passed the group, noticed the dogs, and shouted:

"Sic him, Rags!"

MacGregor whirled on him: "On your way before I close that foolish trap of yours for a week!" The man hurried on.

But a marine echoed the mischievous cry: "Sic him, Jiggs!"

The marine sergeant silenced the man with a growl—"You'll get yours for that."

Rags and Jiggs looked up inquiringly at the trouble-makers and continued their nuzzling. A group of news-picture men who had arrived with the marines indicated impatience to get into action. They snapped the dogs standing in friendly conference and then looked about for other situations that would make good pictures. It was decided to photograph Rags and Jiggs atop the barrel of a captured war cannon. The marines commanded Jiggs to mount it. The bull wasn't designed for high jumping. He tried gamely enough, but after half a dozen failures the marines had to lift him on. They placed him well out on the muzzle. There he found new difficulty. His forward legs were set too far apart for so delicate a job of balancing as the rounded barrel required. He struggled desperately to keep his balance, but slipped down first on one side and then on the other.

As soon as Jiggs was on the gun, Sergeant Mac-Gregor slapped the breach and called to Rags. The terrier got a running start, bounded to the firing-step, climbed to the top of the breach. He walked out part way on the barrel and sat down comfortably to watch Jiggs, who was finding the footing more and more difficult. Suddenly the bull lost his balance and tumbled ignominiously to the ground. Game, he made several futile attempts to get back. He stood, for a moment, whimpering, as if in shame. Rags hopped off the gun and nuzzled him. For a few seconds it looked as if Rags might be whispering in the bulldog's ear. Then, abruptly, he started at a trot, in the direction of the barracks. Jiggs followed a few paces in the rear. Several men made a move to stop them, but MacGregor intervened.

"Let them go," he ordered. "We'll trail along and see what Rags is up to."

They found Rags taking the shortest route to the kitchen of H Company. The mess sergeant was getting ready for the evening meal when the dogs arrived. The terrier trotted up, sat back on his haunches, and lifted his paws.

"What?" said the sergeant. "Hungry in the middle of the day? All right, old-timer, I'll fix you right up."

He gathered a brimming plate of meat and potatoes, and set it, with a pan of water, in front of Rags. The terrier stepped back to Jiggs, edged the bull toward the plate, and sat down to watch him eat.

"Well, I'll be darned!" cried the sergeant. "Rags brought that gyrene dog over here for a handout."

He filled another plate and gave it to Rags, but the terrier nibbled daintily, pausing now and then to turn his one eye on the bull, as if to make certain the guest had everything he wanted. The meal over, Rags led the way back to the cannon. Without waiting for the soldiers and photographers to catch up, he jumped to the firing-step and paused until the bull joined him. Jiggs managed the short leap without much trouble. Rags then climbed to the top of the breach, and Jiggs clumsily followed. Rags stepped easily out toward the end, stopping when Jiggs, following him, found the barrel getting too narrow for his broad-gauge forelegs. There the terrier settled himself comfortably, as if to say to the picture men: "Go ahead and do your stuff."

The terrier's gesture was not lost on the soldiers.

"Rags is sure givin' the leatherneck a break," piped up a young corporal.

"Sure is," grumbled a veteran, "but when it gets into the gyrene history books it'll be the other way found."

"Aw, pipe down!" growled the marine sergeant. "You guys always got the best of it."

"Yeah," chuckled MacGregor, "with the help o' God an' a few marines, not to mention a leatherneck press agent that was a swell fiction-writer!"

"What d'you mean by that?" snapped the marine sergeant. "If we wasn't on duty I'd take a sock ——"

"Boy, this duty ain't permanent," MacGregor cut in. "Any time you feel that way just nominate the place where you can be found—an' leave the names an' addresses of next of kin to be notified."

"Say, you must think you're——"

"Brup! Brup! Brup-erup-erup-erup!"

The interruption came from Rags. He had seen no cameras pointed in his direction—the picture men were enjoying the army-marine debate—and he was getting tired of sitting on the gun. Jiggs was having trouble, too, but was hanging on grimly—slipping a little now and then, but pantingly regaining his balance. Mac-Gregor turned toward the terrier with a laugh.

"Right you are, Rags," he declared. "We're a lot of saps to keep you sitting there while we chew the rag." Then to the marine: "The dog's got more sense than we have. Let's finish up making the pictures and call it a day."

The pictures made, the soldiers lifted both Jiggs and Rags from the gun muzzles. Rags trotted beside the bulldog to the ferry dock and stood as the boat pulled out, in the manner of one making a graceful farewell. When the craft cleared the slip he turned and began a leisurely canter toward home. Once there, he curled up in the living-room, a bit tired from his exertions. Rags was getting on; he no longer had the endurance of the war days, although he was not lacking in pep for short spurts. He was gradually developing a preference for leisurely existence. It was ten years since the war had ended, and that is a long time in the life of a dog. It also makes a difference in men.

Rags appeared to notice the change when, for the first time since he had been carried from the Meuse-Argonne, he began meeting those who had fought with him. The veterans, loyal to their war-time memories, through the workaday grind of civilian life, were gathering for the annual reunion of the First Division. Rags knew many of them, but as they greeted him he cocked his good eye at them doubtfully and sniffed them, Lean, bronzed, hard, and devil-may-care they had been in the old days. Now they were fat, pink-white, seriously concerned with the business of making a living. As one after another they came, Rags acted as if he could hardly believe his nose when it told him they were old friends. To his eye they were a strange lot. Besides, Rags had known them all in uniform. They were in mufti now.

They wandered over the post in little groups, gathering here and there when they met an old comrade who was still in the army. They sang some of the old songs. Rags first heard the singing as he was easing his way into the post exchange. He froze to a stiff attention, his good ear cocked upward, listening. The tune was the same; the words were the ones Rags had heard many a time in the old days. But after listening for a minute he dropped his head and trotted off. The terrier had sensed that something was lacking. The singing wasn't the same as of old. In France it had been the spontaneous outpouring of youthful nonchalance, indifferent to death or privation. It rang true. Now it sounded like a group of solid citizens telling themselves they still believed in Santa Claus. Rags paid no further attention to it, although he continued to hunt out old friends as they reported at the island.

As the convention got under way he found a new interest. Down on the parade-ground the terrier sighted a clump of uniforms, with a group of picture men ling up their cameras. He galloped down and, to the dismay of several junior officers, bounded up to a short, slim soldier in the uniform of a major-general. Before the juniors could tear him away the general was scratching his head and talking to him.

"Well, old fellow," he said, "I've heard a lot about you lately, but this is the first time I've seen you in years."

"I didn't know the general knew the dog," an aide explained, apologetically.

"Oh yes," said General Summerall. "We met on the other side. I've been intending to look Rags up."

"How about taking his picture with the generals?" a camera man inquired.

Rags stepped back from General Summerall and looked around as if to say: "Generals? My word! Have we more than one?"

There were, as a matter of fact, three—General Summerall, Major-General Frank Parker, and Major General Robert Lee Bullard. All had at one time or another commanded the First Division and all had come to attend the reunion. The generals had no objection to being photographed with the division mascot.

"Why not?" said General Bullard. "Why not?" other generals echoed. Several sergeants who were on the sidelines heard the proposal and raced for the storeroom where the banner telling of Rags's record was kept. Another whispered to the picture men to delay the proceedings until it could be fetched. In a few moments the banner was set up and Rags was placed on a chair in front of it. The generals, a beribboned sergeant, and some former division members were ranged on either side.

"Looks like they're taking a picture of the generals with the dog, instead of a picture of the dog with the generals?" a supercilious young aide complained.

"And why not?" snapped General Bullard. There were no more comments. The picture—probably the only one in which an army dog was given the position of honor by the highest ranking general officers in the army—was made without a hitch. Rags sat as if being photographed with generals for flankers was an everyday affair with him. He appeared just a little bored.

Soon after the reunion the Hardenbergh family began preparations for moving. The major had been ordered to the War College at Washington, D. C. Rags appeared surprised. It was a long time since the family had moved, and the terrier seemed to have made up this mind that the moving days had come to an end. He entered into the plan with gusto, however, giving every indication that he was perfectly happy to see a little more of the world. As the family supervised the work of packing he was continually at the heels of one or another. Occasionally he turned up his good eye inquiringly, as if seeking assurance that he would be taken along as usual. Apparently satisfied, he set about making his farewells, as had been his custom in the past. Nor did he confine himself to Governors Island.

He waited for the Fort Hamilton boat, and put in a day there. Then, remembering the engineers down at Fort Hancock, he slipped aboard the mine-planter and paid them a farewell visit. A few days later the military police at the ferry landing reported that they were having a time keeping Rags off the boat. For two days, they said, he had exerted all sorts of wiles in attempts to get aboard. They were afraid he'd finally succeed, sometime in a crowd, and would somebody please do something about it?

Sergeant MacGregor guessed what was in Rags's mind.

"You know what's up?" he told his mates at mess, between husky mouthfuls of steak, "the little tike knows he's leavin' the island, an' he wants to say goodbye to the gang over at 39 Whitehall."

"Why don't you take him over?" the stable sergeant inquired.

"I will. But how the darned little pup remembers beats me. It's been about three years since he's over there."

"Don't believe Rags ever forgets anythin'."

"Sure is a great little pup. Terriers are funny, anyhow."

Before MacGregor got a chance to help Rags make his call at the Army Building, the major was ready to start for Washington. As the cab whisked him through lower Broadway on the way to the train the terrier recognized the location and, sticking his head out of the cab window, barked his farewell toward the old red Army Building he could not see.

CHAPTER SEVENTEEN
WAR COLLEGE

THE Army War College is an unusual sort of school. It is probably the only educational plant in the country where virtually all the students have graying hair. Majors, lieutenant-colonels and colonels attend its classes. They study harder than the cadets at West Point. The course probably is the most difficult and intense known. Yet, somehow, a certain schoolboy spirit permeates the place. At recess the officers play as hard as any group of youngsters in a village school. Dignified colonels, in their shirt sleeves, pitch horseshoes, play leapfrog and baseball, and cavort about the playground, which is hidden behind the college building, on the toe of a spit of land jutting into the Potomac. Walls and other buildings shield the players from the public gaze. Only students, or their friends, are admitted. Officers, who in their youth were "big league" baseball material, fumble grounders, muff flies, and strike out against pitching a nine of sandlot kids would welcome with home runs, although the pitchers once were college stars. But they all enjoy it. It provides relaxation from the study grind.

Rags, a few days after his arrival, discovered the playground. Many of the officers had been with the first Division in France. All had heard of the terrier. They wound up their ball game to entertain him. A Colonel called him, showed him a baseball, and then 'flung it with a cry of, "Go fetch, Rags!"

Rags fixed his good eye on the colonel, straightened his tail in mid-wag, turned about, walked over to a corner of the wall, and lay down.

"Huh!" grunted the colonel. "Don't want to play, it seems."

Several officers junior to the colonel grinned. They knew Rags' views on fetching and carrying. But they didn't bother to explain. The baseball game was resumed, with Rags on the sidelines, now and then encouraging the runners with barks. After the recess Rags went home— the major was living outside the preservation, but the terrier quickly learned the way. The family tried to discourage his visits to the War College. There was a regulation that all dogs on the reservation must be muzzled. They didn't like to muzzle Rags. The nearest thing to a muzzle he ever had worn was a gas mask. But Rags continued to visit the College as the spirit moved him. The soldiers who policed the place knew his history, so they looked the other way when he came ambling along with jaws untrammeled. Once the general commanding the college met him. Rags trotted up to him, sniffed him, and made signs of friendship.

"Humph!" said the general. "Unmuzzled. Violation of orders! Humph!"

He stooped to read the terrier's collar, seeking the identity of the owner who had presumed to disobey his order. If he was in the army—well, he'd be taught that orders were orders. The general found the name-plate almost concealed by Rags's fuzzy coat.

"First Division Rags!" he read aloud. "Humph!"

The general had heard of Rags, but never had met him. Nevertheless, the laurels that had made the officer a general had been won with the First Division at Cantigny, before Rags had joined it. He scratched the terrier's neck and patted his head.

"First Division, eh? Humph!" he commented, and strode on. Nobody ever heard anything—from the general—about Rags running loose without a muzzle.

In his wanderings in Potomac Park, Rags was less fortunate. District of Columbia regulations as to muzzling of dogs are strict. A motorcycle cop in the park nabbed Rags—actually arrested him and took him to police headquarters. The cop was kindly, gentle as could be, but firm. Rags eyed him suspiciously at first, sniffed him, and then began to treat the cop as a long lost friend. All would have been well if Rags had a license tag. He didn't. Some small boys had stolen it to fasten to their own mongrel pet. Rags hadn't objected. The dangling tag annoyed him. He submitted to the theft as if he felt they were doing him a favor. At the police station the cop explained his views to the captain.

"No muzzle an' no tag," he said, "but I hate to send the little fellow to the pound. I knew a chap in France had a dog just like this—signal corps guy named Donovan. I heard him an' the pup got it at Meuse-Argonne. But this little pooch looks just like the one Donovan had. I'd like to take him home for the kids."

"Okay with me," the captain agreed, and strolled from his desk to look the terrier over. "He's got a collar. There was a tag on it, too. Somebody must o' swiped it. Collar's got a plate."

The captain pushed Rags toward the light so that he could read the lettering on his collar. Then he straightened up.

"What was the name of that dog your friend Donovan had?" he inquired.

The cop scratched his head: "Gee! I've forgot. Lemme think. ... I got it. ... They called him 'Rags.'"

"Uh-huh! Take a squint at this fellow's collar. It says 'First Division Rags' on it."

The cop looked, and then examined Rags more closely. He noticed the blind eye, the crippled ear. Then: "Guess him an' Donovan must of pulled through, after all. Prob'ly Donovan's stationed here somewheres."

"Call up the army and find out."

The policeman glanced at the clock. It lacked a few minutes of six.

"Too late," he said. "They shut up shop at four-thirty. We'll see about Donovan in the morning."

"Well, we might as well let the dog go home," the captain decided.

They turned Rags out with the admonition to "Go home." The terrier, once in the street, gazed blankly about him. He had never been in that part of the city before. He stood on the corner, uncertainly, for a few minutes, watching automobiles tearing along both streets at the intersection. Then he went back into police headquarters.

"He doesn't want to go home," the cop who had arrested Rags opined. "Maybe he's fixin" to stay with us."

"Yeah, an' maybe he don't know the way," the captain guessed.

"I noticed him as I came in," another policeman volunteered. "It looked to me like he was scared o' the gas-wagons."

The captain took Rags to the street and helped him across through the traffic. Still Rags made no move to depart. A tall soldierly man came along. His walrus-like mustache was snow-white. So was the hair visible below the brim of his black slouch hat. He carried a blackthorn stick and strode along like a man of fifty, although well past the seventy mark. The police captain saluted him.

"Good evening, General," he greeted. "Walking a bit late this evening?"

"Never too late to walk. Trouble with people nowadays is they don't walk enough. Each generation seems to be getting weaker. Can't see that it gets any wiser."

"Guess you're right, General; guess you're right. We certainly don't get the men we used to."

"Humph! Know I'm right. Can't move troops across the street now without transportation. When I was a captain soldiers carried their transportation with 'em, by gad! at the end o' their legs. They marched. An' they were hard. Now look at 'em. What's wrong with the dog?"

"He don't seem to want to go home, sir."

"Humph! Probably doesn't know the way. Where's he live?"

"I don't know, General."

"Don't know, an' you're tryin' to send him home. Huh! Didn't you ever learn that 'fore you can get a dog—or a horse—to do what you want

103

you've got to know more than they do?"

"Guess you're right, General; guess you're right."

"Know I'm right. Seen it tried hundreds o' times. Where'd the little fellow come from? Whose dog is he?"

Briefly the police captain outlined the story of Rags's arrest, explaining also the discovery that he had been the First Division mascot in France.

"But we can't find out where Donovan is, General, so we don't know where to take Rags," he concluded.

"Huh!" growled the general. "Don't you ever read the papers? Donovan's dead. Dog's on the army retired list—like myself. Attached himself to a Major Something-or-other—I forget the name. Major's down here at the War College. It was all in the papers."

"Funny I didn't see it, General."

"Can't see things in the papers if you don't read 'em. Turn him over to me. I'll get him home."

"Does the General remember where the officer lives?"

"No, I don't—never knew. But I remember something about dogs. Little fellow's never been in this part o' town before. Can't get his bearings. Thing to do is take him where he knows the lay o' the land. Then he'll get home without any trouble."

"I can send him back to where they found him in the park, sir."

"Don't bother. I'll take care of him. C'm here, Rags!"

Rags, who had been eyeing the general, obeyed promptly and stood before the old man at a stiff attention, as if saying, "I know a general when I see one."

The general signaled a passing taxicab, lifted Rags in, and climbed in himself.

"War College," he ordered.

The taxi cabby pulled his flag, then thoughtfully turned to his passenger.

"It's all closed up at this hour," he explained. "You won't find nobody there."

"I know it," snapped the general. "What of it? Drive where you're told."

The driver grunted, but obeyed. The general talked to Rags.

"Hate to ride in these infernal things," he explained to the terrier. "Fellow that invented them ought to have been hanged 'fore he did. Just have to use 'em, though. Isn't any place any more where you can drive a decent horse. You'd kill a good horse on these blasted pavements."

Rags cocked up his good ear attentively and placed a paw on the general's knee.

"You wouldn't believe it," the old man went on, "but you can't find a young fellow of twenty-one nowadays that can hitch up a horse, much less drive one. They can all drive these confounded machines, though, drat 'em! Don't know anything about horses an' dogs. You'd think anybody'd know a dog couldn't get his bearings when you set him down in a totally strange place. Not these days. Mechanical age. Automobiles an' airplanes an' movies—Livin' in pigeonhole flats that wouldn't hold a good-sized Saratoga trunk—No home cookin' any more—no homes, I guess—If all the can-openers got lost the country'd starve to death."

The old general rambled on, voicing the resentment of age against the changes that have banished the familiar things of other days. The driver swung up in front of the War College and stopped with a screech of brakes.

"Here you are, sir. War College, sir."

"All right. Wait," said the general as he lifted Rags out. "Go home, Rags," he ordered.

The terrier glanced about him, got his bearings, and, after a few barks and flourishes of tail, very plainly saying "thank you," set off at an easy lope down the drive.

"Follow that dog," the general ordered his driver. "Go slow and don't scare him."

Rags took a short cut, but the cab picked him up again at the edge of the grounds and trailed him until he turned into a house. At the gate Rags waited expectantly. But the general did not stop.

"New Hampshire apartments," he ordered.

Rags watched until the tail-light of the cab disappeared around the corner. Then, slowly and a bit regretfully, he approached the door and scratched for admission.

The general, on arriving home, telephoned a most influential Senator and explained the trouble that had been visited on Rags. The Senator agreed that such things should not be. He would do something about it—unofficially at first. If that didn't solve the difficulty, he'd see about having some official action taken. It wasn't necessary. The police themselves had passed the word along. Rags, muzzle or not, with tag or without, was assured the freedom of the capital.

He needed it, too, for the day after his meeting with the old general he developed a fever of restless activity. First he virtually called the roll at the War College. Next day he took a census of the reservation, nosing his way into the quarters of every officer on the place. Then he extended his activities to neighboring posts—to the State, War and Navy building itself. Until a policeman casually told an army sergeant about Rags's meeting with the old general, the terrier's behavior caused his friends some concern. But as the story finally filtered through to the War College personnel a great light broke over them.

"He's trying to find the Old Man," they decided. "Smart dog, all right. Evidently knows the old boy is army."

"He was once, and HOW!" cut in a colonel. "He was the whole bloomin' army. Believe me, when he was running it, they stepped around."

"Funny how a hard-boiled old walrus like that would go to so much trouble for a dog," a young major, who had entered the army after the general's retirement, observed.

"He always loved horses and dogs," a lieutenant-colonel explained. "Always had 'em, too. When I was a shavetail the Old Boy owned the best trotters in this part of the country."

"Do you suppose he'll drop around to see the dog?" the young major asked the speaker.

"Not him. He'd like to, you can bet. But he doesn't approve of our modern ways. Says we turn out softies instead of soldiers. Then he never approved of the General Staff much. I'm afraid he'll never get over here."

"Might be a good idea to take Rags to see him."

"Sure, if you were invited. But you can't go dropping in on generals so-so, you know. And the Old Man is still boo-coop general, even if he is retired."

"He hasn't got any grudge against the service, has he?"

"Absolutely not. He's fond of us all as individual soldiers. He's always dealing out little gifts to the younger officers he likes. Only today the chap who was up here with those First Division trucks from Fort Jay told me the Old Man had given him the finest bridle and saddle and blanket he'd ever laid eyes on."

"Not such a bad old duffer after all, eh?"

"At heart he's a prince. But he's salty and snappy—the habit of command, you know."

Rags, who had been watching the speakers with his good ear uppermost, got up, stretched and ambled off. As he trotted down the drive he passed a parked train of First Division trucks. A lone soldier was guarding them. Rags had known him at Governors Island and paused to exchange greetings. Suddenly the little terrier sniffed, looked inquiringly at the man, and sniffed again.

"What's the matter?" the guard asked. "Cats?"

Rags ran to one of the trucks, sniffed some more, then, with a running leap, landed aboard and began smelling a beautifully finished saddle, a silver-mounted bridle, and a rich-looking blanket, which were piled in the rear. He barked sharply as if trying to ask a question. The soldier looked at him quizzically.

"That's the stuff the old fellow gave the cap'n," he explained. "What's wrong with it?"

Rags stopped barking and settled down on the blanket.

"Want to wait for the skipper?" the soldier asked. "Okay. Make yourself comfortable."

The soldier curled up on a seat to finish reading his magazine. Rags settled down in the truck, obviously intending to wait until the man whose scent he had caught on the articles appeared. He fell asleep. The soldier forgot about him.

CHAPTER EIGHTEEN
HITCH HIKING

RAGS was sleeping when the officer waved the truck train into motion. The roar of the motors and the bumping of the vehicle as it got under way awakened him. He sniffed the saddle again, looked out over the tailboard; then settled back to his nap. The rolling and swaying lulled him. The truck train was thundering over the Conowengo highway, when the terrier finally awakened. He looked out, poised as if about to jump, hesitated, and lay down again. The trucks moved at top speed. The officer was planning to reach Governors Island for breakfast. Rags lay still while a few more miles rolled behind. Then he clambered over the material to the front of the truck and barked loudly at the driver. The man turned, saw the dog, and signaled with his horn that the captain was wanted. The other drivers repeated the signal until it reached the leader. He stopped. A sergeant clambered down and walked back to the truck that carried Rags.

"Captain's gone ahead in his own car," he announced. "What's botherin' you?"

"I got a hitch-hiker," the driver explained. "What'll I do about it?"

"Let him ride, or kick him off. Who cares?"

"But it's a dog—Rags. You remember him—the little pup that used to be down at the island."

"Sure I know him. How'd he get on this truck?"

"Search me!" Then, remembering suddenly, he told of Rags's actions on the drive at the War College. "He seemed all het up about that stuff the old feller gave the skipper, an' crawled in with it. I guess I must o' forgot about him."

"Guess. No guessin' about it. You did. You was so entranced to find out whether Flossie Flatfoot married the hero an' lived happy ever after, in that slush you're always readin', that you didn't check your load. You just threw 'er in an' highballed."

"Gee! Sarge, you couldn't expect me to know the little pup would stick with us."

"I don't expect you to know anythin'. If brains was money you couldn't buy a breakfast for a flea."

The sergeant walked around and spoke to Rags.

"General's all gone," he explained, tapping the saddle and spreading his hands in a gesture of emptiness. "You won't find him here."

Rags fixed his good eye on the sergeant. Then he slowly walked to the tailboard. The sergeant repeated his remark and the gesture. Rags stiffly hopped to the ground and started dejectedly back down the road at a slow lope.

"Hey, Rags!" the sergeant called. "Come back here. You can't hoof it home!"

Rags kept on going.

"Rags!" There was the ring of authority in the sergeant's voice—it was the one he used to recalcitrant soldiers. Rags stopped and waited. The sergeant hurried down the road and picked him up.

"You'll have to go on in with us," he explained. "Then we'll send you back somehow." He turned to the driver. "I'll take care o' Rags. But you'd better be careful an elephant or a camel don't stow away on you, dumbbell."

With Rags under his arm he trudged ahead to the leading truck, lifted Rags to a pile of blankets, and climbed in.

"Let 'er roll," he ordered. "I'll ride back here an' make sure nothin' more happens to Rags."

The terrier curled up with a gesture of resignation as the train got under way again. Tire trouble caused considerable delay, but he slept until a halt was made for breakfast, just outside of Trenton. The sergeant shared some sandwiches with him, and gave him water in a meat-can, just as Donovan used to do. It was a long time since Rags had sampled field rations. He barked, wagged his tail appreciatively, and fell to.

"Fifteen minutes," the sergeant warned the soldiers. "We're due in now, an' we've got to make it by noon if we have to run these ol' relics in on flats."

"Relics is right," cut in a corporal. "I bet you every one o' these ol' rattletraps has got wound stripes."

"Sure. All I'm glad about is that they didn't have no motor-trucks in the Civil War."

"How come? Motors beat horses; or mules."

"Right. But horses an' mules die once in a while an' have to be replaced. If a survey officer's got any doubt about 'em bein' no more use, his nose'll tell him in a couple o' days. Motors is different. If they was motortrucks in the Civil War, they'd expect the army to keep 'em runnin' still. Time's up. Powder your pretty noses an' start rollin'."

The sergeant guided the train over little-used thoroughfares and avoided traffic congestion until forced to swing into the arterial highway that would bring him to a ferry for downtown New York. It was exactly noon when the first of the trucks chugged onto Governors Island, from the ferryboat General Humphreys. Several trips were required to bring all of them. The captain was waiting impatiently at the dock.

"Welcome, strangers!" he greeted, sarcastically. "I suppose you just couldn't tear yourselves away from the beautiful scenery?"

"Tire trouble, sir," the sergeant explained. "Some o' the rubber on these antiques suddenly remembered its age."

The captain laughed. He knew those ancient vehicles as well as the sergeant.

"Stop for breakfast?" he inquired.

"Yes, sir. Fifteen minutes."

"Everything okay?"

"Yes, sir. 'Cept we seem to have collected a deserter—or an A. W. O. L. Don't know which."

"Let's have a look at him."

Rags, who had been lying quietly in the truck, suddenly hopped out and trotted toward them.

"Here he comes now, sir," the sergeant explained. "It's Rags, the Division Mascot. He smuggled himself aboard in Washington and we didn't notice him until we were way past Baltimore."

"Hum! Why in thunder don't these fellows police their trucks. We've got to wire the major, and then we've got to send the little hobo back."

"I couldn't put him down on the road, sir."

"Of course not. Has he been fed?"

"Yes, sir. Split up my ration with him."

"Good. I'll have to see the chief about sending him back. Hello, Rags!"

The terrier answered the greeting with a bark and a twitch of his tail. Then he trotted up the incline and headed toward the barracks. He met Sergeant MacGregor coming out of H Company's quarters, and lifted up his voice when still a couple of rods away. The sergeant glanced casually toward the barking; paused in his walk and looked more closely. Then he turned toward the barracks and shouted:

"Turn out, you chair-polishers. Look who's here!"

In a few minutes there was a ring of soldiers around Rags, patting him, scratching him, and telling him what a fine dog he was.

Meanwhile, plans were being made to send him back to the War College. A general check-up revealed that no army folk were going to Washington within the next few days. Not even an army plane was flying down. The inquiry was extended to the navy. A crack naval pilot was flying a big amphibian to the Washington Navy Yard, solo, and if the army would send an escort, Rags could go along.

Corporal Miller, with a forty-eight hour pass in his pocket, volunteered as guardian. Less than two hours after Rags's arrival at Governors Island he was in the cockpit of the amphibian, which was racing across the water for a take-off. The terrier looked inquiringly at Miller as the motor roared. He stood a bit nervously, his nose against the corporal, when the plane bucked and leaped in the swell of a liner. He shifted uneasily as it soared, circled for altitude, turned south, and headed for Washington as the crow flies.

For the first half hour of flying Rags nestled close to the corporal's feet. Then he twisted and wriggled in the cramped cockpit until he got his paws on Miller's knees. His good ear was cocked upward and his sharp face wore a puzzled expression. Miller lifted him to his lap, snapped a leash on his collar, tied the leash to the safety belt and then permitted Rags to poke his nose over the edge of the plane. The moment the terrier caught the rush of wind he drew back, threw himself from the corporal's lap and flattened himself against the floor. He looked at Miller expectantly. The corporal grinned at him. He had heard of Rags's battlefield tricks and knew what the terrier was thinking.

"That's not shell blast, old fellow," he explained, bending low in the cockpit, so his voice could be heard above the roar of the motor. "You're travelin' about a hundred miles an hour—that's what makes the wind."

Rags got up and was again lifted to the corporal's lap. Gingerly he poked his nose over the edge, first on one side, then on the other. He stretched out a little farther and looked down. He noticed the shadow of the plane on the water of the Delaware River and barked vigorously at it. A choppy wind came up and the ride turned bumpy. The pilot was working like a Trojan to keep the ship even. He turned and signaled for less activity in the rear cockpit. So the corporal lifted Rags to the floor again and urged him to be still. After a few minutes of futile coaxing for another peep over the side, Rags curled up and went to sleep. The roar of the motor didn't seem to bother him. He did not awaken until the amphibian drifted to a bobbing stop in the water off the War College.

Back on land, Rags barked and wagged his thanks to the corporal and the pilot. Then he started across the grounds as nonchalantly as if he was returning from a mere constitutional trot around the block. There was nothing in his manner to indicate he had just completed what, for a dog, was a rather unusual adventure. As he swung down the drive, Rags slackened his pace and surveyed a dog some fifty yards ahead—a bull terrier. It had arrived with a captain while Rags was traveling to Governors Island. Rags did not stop. But he moved warily with one eye on the bull, tail swaying in a friendship signal, and trotted past the fighting dog as if he had scarcely seen him. The bull's tail started vibrating in sympathy as the sleek white battler turned and trotted amicably alongside Rags. It wore a muzzle. Rags stopped as a boyish voice called:

"Here, Rags! Here Rags! C'mere, John L.!"

It was the son of the captain. Rags had known him at Governors Island. He waited for the youngster to catch up.

The boy—about nine years old—came at a run, lifted one of Rags's paws and one of the bull's.

"Rags, meet John L.," he introduced. "John L., this is Rags, an' if he needs any fightin' done, you do it."

He placed the dogs' paws together and shook them solemnly.

"Now you two are sworn friends," he explained. Then he removed the muzzle from John L. "You stick with Rags," he advised. "Nobody makes him wear a muzzle, an' if you're with him maybe they won't bother you."

The boy turned to Rags.

"Bruce is gone," he said, sadly. Bruce was a Black Aberdeen Rags had known at Governors Island. "The chow killed him. Then father got John L. John L. fixed that chow, didn't you, John L.? You stay friends with him, Rags. He can lick any dog, anywheres. Can't you, John L.?"

The bull looked up and wagged an assurance that he could.

From one of the houses down the row the boy's name was called. He left the dogs and ran toward home, shouting, shrilly: "Coming!" Rags and John L. started toward the gate. They turned into the road to avoid a couple of colonels on the sidewalk.

"What do you know about that?" one of the officers observed. "Rags has gone and dug himself up a bodyguard."

"That bull's some guard, too. Down at Jay he chased all the dogs he didn't like into hiding. Funny how Rags makes friends with other dogs."

"He can fight, too, when he has to. Gettin' pretty old now, though."

"Yes. He must be over twelve. It's going on eleven years since the war ended. But he's pretty spry yet."

The officers passed on. Rags led the terrier to the major's quarters and gave his usual tap on the door. The major opened it and looked him over with a cold, reproving eye.

"So," he said. "You not only go A. W. O. L., but you bring company home with you and expect us to kill the fatted calf, eh!"

Rags sat back on his tail and lifted his paws, as if to say:

"True enough; but please don't scold me in front of my company!"

The major grinned. Rags was a bit of a trial at times, but he never was a bore. One way or another he managed to break up the monotony of life, not only for himself, but for his friends. They would not have had him different. The bull was made welcome and after dinner settled comfortably beside the fireplace, apparently discussing with Rags whatever it is dogs discuss. The captain's young son finally came for him. With a boy's ability to read the minds of his canine friends the youngster had surmised, when John L. failed to appear for his dinner, that he was visiting Rags.

The friendship between Rags and the bull turned out to be an asset to both. John L. was caught in Potomac Park without his muzzle and a couple of policemen were arresting him when Rags intervened. The bull had been resisting valiantly until Rags came up. Then he became quiet. Rags sat up and begged. At first the policemen didn't understand. But when they got John L. in a motorcycle side car and Rags tried to get in too, a light broke over them.

"Must be a friend of yours, Rags," one of the cops remarked.

Rags barked and wagged an emphatic affirmative and again tried to climb into the car.

"All right, then," said the cop, "if you feel that way about it; but take him home out o' here. Git!"

Neither dog stood on ceremony. The terrier appeared to realize he had escaped something unpleasant. Rags, who never forgot, knew. The pair of them streaked it, as fast as they could go, toward the safety of the War College reservation.

A few days later John L. returned the favor. The dogs had wandered to Fort Myer on an exploring expedition. Rags, as always on such missions, was well in the lead. They entered the reservation, circled around it, and finally located the stables. In an open corral were a number of horses. Rags liked horses and began squeezing through a little space in the gate, presumably to strike up a more intimate acquaintance. It was a tight squeeze, and when he was about halfway through, a big police dog came roaring down on him. Rags could neither wriggle all the way through to safety, nor back out to put up a fight, before the hostile dog was upon him. He was helpless. One snap of the big wolfish jaws would have broken his back. But the snap never came.

With a low growl John L. flung himself at the police dog, and

113

stopped the big fellow in mid-stride. The bull was giving away twice his own weight, but that meant nothing to him. Fighting was his business—as the police dog soon found out. By the time Rags had backed himself out of the gate space and turned to aid John L. the police dog had managed to shake the bull off and was streaking it down the road with his tail between his legs. John L. didn't pursue—merely flung a few contemptuous growls after his retreating adversary as if to say, "Next time I'll get real rough with you."

CHAPTER NINETEEN
HELPING THE OLD GANG

THE major's work at the War College was finished as the time for the reunion of the First Division rolled around in November, 1929. He was ordered to Fort Hamilton. The news was greeted with cheers by the division men—present and former. It was the tenth gathering since the men of Meuse-Argonne, Soissons, and other hot battles had been mustered out, and the committee was exerting itself to make it a "rip-snorter." Plans were afoot to promote the largest assemblage since the war. Arrangements were made for a sham battle—a reproduction of one of the hot moments of the old days. The division was to be presented formally with its battle streamers. Summerall, its old chief, now a full general with four stars on his shoulders—the fifth to hold the rank in the history of the army—was to review both the regular army and the veterans.

The presence of Rags made the affair complete. Soldiers rehearsed daily, until they were drilled to a fine point. A big Broadway parade was planned. There were to be receptions. The world was to be reminded that the spirit of the First Division was very much alive. Somehow, the message didn't get out to the world. The usual notices were sent to the newspapers, but they didn't get printed. It was a bad time for reunions. The stock market in Wall Street was having the most sensational crash in its history. Stocks which had been regarded as gilt-edged were dropping as much as twenty points in an hour of trading. Newspapers issued hourly extras shrieking the latest bad news from the "Street." There were a couple of spectacular murders, with the elements of mystery that the public dotes on. The United States was being urged to sink its navy. There was war in China, war talk in the Balkans, and rumors of a couple of revolutions in South America. Frantic editors were trying to make room for all the news they regarded as "red hot." One of them would glance at the notice of the First Division's reunion and toss it aside when a copy boy laid the latest Wall Street bulletin on his desk. Then he would forget about it while he wrote a new headline stating that International Flying Goose, Inc., had dropped another forty points.

"Reunions we have always with us," was the general view. Nobody had time to realize that the First Division really was an unusual outfit. A wandering photographer did notice the activity at Fort Hamilton. He also discovered Rags, and took a picture of the terrier with Brigadier-General

Hugh A. Drum, commander of the First Division. The newspapers printed the picture —they always printed Rags's picture—but they didn't say much about the reunion. It looked as if the First was going to have a rather private party, all by itself. But its members carried on with the old game spirit. They planned and drilled and perfected their program with as much care as if the rest of the world was to be on the side lines.

Rags observed the proceedings with acute interest. For hours he would linger along the edge of the parade-ground, watching the soldiers march and countermarch, in preparation for the presentation of the streamers; or doing skirmish practice, getting ready for the sham battle. There was no firing in the skirmish practice. The men merely learned their places and moved to establish the time required for the maneuver. Occasionally there was a gallery of civilians. And it was a woman member of this group that finally broke up a parade and caused Rags no end of annoyance.

The woman had been watching from a small automobile. She had driven it over the edge of the parade-ground to get a better view. H Company, from Governors Island, was swinging along on a platoon front. Her car was in the way. An officer requested her to move it. The approach of the troops in cadence apparently excited her. She jammed the shift into reverse and stepped on the gas with all her strength. The car slithered backward just as the front line of troops arrived. It kept going, in a ragged semicircle, and was bearing down on Rags when Sergeant MacGregor saw it. The auto was on the terrier's blind and deaf side and Rags didn't notice it. He was watching the soldiers. MacGregor threw discipline to the winds, broke ranks, and dashed for the dog. So did half a dozen other old soldiers. They snatched him out of the way, barely in time. The lieutenant leading the platoon caught the break in the rhythm, glanced around, saw what was going on, and ordered a halt.

MacGregor carried Rags to safety and with the others resumed his place in the line. The officer surveyed his command again and resumed the march without comment. He knew Rags's story. It was perhaps the only time in army history that discipline had been knocked into a cocked hat without a single official comment on the matter.

Rags, as the parade passed on, ran along surveying the crowd on the side lines. There were perhaps a dozen automobiles which had been driven up over the curb so their occupants could get a better view. The terrier stopped in front of each one and sniffed disapprovingly. Then he turned his back on the parade-ground and headed down toward the waterfront. It was plain that he didn't like to have automobiles chasing him, right on his own post.

Meantime, a reserve officer who saw Rags's rescue told a policeman about it. The policeman passed the information along to a newspaperman. The reporter regarded the business as a pretty fair story. So did the editors. Next morning groups of officers at the various posts found headlines blaring the account of Rags's narrow escape at them.

"What do you know about that?" a colonel inquired. "Here we've been moving heaven and earth to get the news about this reunion in the paper and Rags puts it over without even trying."

"Gosh!" spoke up a gloomy-looking officer. "The poor old First is in a tough fix when it has to depend on Rags for a little space in the newspapers."

"Yeah?" shot back the colonel. "If I'm not losin' my memory, there was one time when part of the First Division depended on him for more than that— in Meuse-Argonne."

The gloomy one grinned:

"Come to think of it, you're right. I was with the outfit that was doing the depending."

A lieutenant came in and addressed himself to the colonel.

"The newspapers are burning up my telephone," he explained. "They want to know what about this rescue of Rags."

"It's correct the way they've got it."

"But they want an interview with the general about it."

"Well?"

"He's busy."

"That seems to be the answer."

"But they want to know if anybody's going to be court-martialed for breaking ranks."

"Tell 'em we're going to shoot the whole bunch at sunrise tomorrow—and to have some photographers on hand."

The lieutenant grinned. Then, seriously: "But I've really got to tell 'em something. Can't afford to get 'em sore, with the reunion an' everything."

"Then tell 'em that it's not the custom in the army to punish men for breaking ranks to save a comrade's life. Tell 'em Rags is the ranking veteran of the division and that the men will be commended."

Along about noon automobiles began arriving at the division headquarters and picture men and reporters clambered out of them. They wanted pictures of the general and Rags; they wanted pictures of the men who had rescued Rags; they wanted an interview with the general.

The pictures of the rescuers could not be obtained. No officer had taken official notice of the men who had fallen out of ranks. And, as Sergeant MacGregor put it, "We'd do it again for Rags, but we ain't makin' any permanent record for the leathernecks to horselaugh the undisciplined doughboys with."

The officers explained the soldiers' viewpoint to the camera men, who glumly conceded there was justice in it. The reporters talked to the general, who gave them the history of the division from first to last. Meanwhile, half a dozen soldiers were detailed to hunt up Rags. Seeking the little terrier on the big reservation was like hunting a pin in a feather bed. There were any number of places he might be. The only way to be sure of him was to catch him early in the morning—at the major's house—and keep him until the photographers could get around.

"Well, wouldn't he come home for supper? We can make flashlight pictures," the camera men announced.

He might and he might not. Officers explained the terrier's habit of dropping in on his various friends at mealtime. The post might be searched from one end to the other without finding him. But the picture men were assured that Rags would be available next day.

"Doggone it!" grumbled a young camera man. "You'd think the darned pooch was J. P. Morgan or somebody. Just about as hard to shoot."

"Somebody is right," rasped a photographer with a silver World War button in his lapel. "If you'd been through what that little pup's been through you'd think you were somebody. You'd probably want to run for President."

"Well, I don't see why we have to cool our heels all day for a darned dog—even if he did get shot up in the war."

"Huh! Shot up is right. An' I don't see why Rags should sit around waiting for a lot o' news-camera stiffs. He don't read the newspapers."

"You comin' back tomorrow?"

"Dunno. I'm goin' to tell the boss just how she lays. It's up to him."

"Aw, I'm goin' to throw it down. I ain't comin' out here to the little end o' nowhere just to shoot a pooch. I can't see anything in it. We got a million dog pictures in the files now."

"Well, my boss thinks it's good stuff. So do I."

The men separated to drive homeward. Those at the fort saw them depart regretfully. They wished Rags had stayed around where he could be photographed.

"Rags made a swell start as a press agent," commented a first lieutenant, "but he didn't follow it up. Somebody'll shoot somebody over in New York tonight and they'll forget all about our reunion by morning."

"Or the stock market'll take another toboggan ride," put in a captain.

"Oh, I don't know," a second lieutenant remarked. "They seemed pretty well interested. What's the mad haste about having the picture today?"

"There you go," moaned the first speaker, who had been a newspaper reporter before the war. "Where haven't I heard those words before, when the papers wanted some army news hot off the griddle. What's the mad rush? Won't tomorrow do? Ye gods! I wish every officer in the army had to put in a year in a newspaper madhouse before he's commissioned."

"Well, I don't see why it was such a matter of life and death getting that picture tonight."

"You wouldn't. And I'm afraid that Rags has associated with this man's army so long, that he's got the same notion. We've muffed a swell chance for publicity for the reunion.

"I'll bet they'll be back tomorrow."

"A good cigar they are not."

The first lieutenant lost his bet. Bright and early the next morning a crowd of photographers was at Division headquarters waiting for Rags. Among them was the youngster who the day before had announced his intention to "throw it down."

"Well, I see you didn't throw hard enough, Bright Eyes," the photographer with the silver war button greeted.

"Oh, I had it killed, all right, but they got a new angle. The Borough President of Brooklyn is sending Rags an invitation to visit Borough Hall. They've framed up a big send-off for him."

"Well, I've seen a lot o' bozos get a big hand at Borough Hall—an' City Hall, too—that didn't have it comin' as much as Rags."

"I suppose so. Wonder how much longer we've got to hang around here."

"Can't do anything until the messenger from Borough Hall gets here with the invitation."

"What we goin' to do? Shoot him handin' it to the pooch?"

"That's the idea. We'll get the general an' a couple o' these old-timers with plenty o' ribbons. It'll make a swell shot."

The messenger from the Borough President finally arrived. There were introductions all around and the camera men set up their apparatus, ready for action. Inside the division office, a sweating lieutenant was frantically telephoning:

"But, Major, we've got to have him—But I promised last night—But you were informed, you know, to keep him there—You say he wasn't home last night?—Can something have happened to him?—Good Lord! What'll I tell the newspaper men—I'll have to tell the chief first—Any idea of where he might be?—Well, we'll have to find him, that's all— G'-by."

The young officer was pale and nervous as he stepped to the porch of the division headquarters. He cleared his throat nervously.

"Gentlemen," he began, "I don't just know how to tell you, after all the trouble you've been put to, b-b-but Rags has disappeared. We haven't any idea of where he is."

"Okay," piped up a veteran reporter who lolled against a pillar. "Good publicity stunt, Lieutenant, 'cept you don't need it today. Save it. The reunion'll get plenty space. Trot out the pup an' let's interview him."

"But, seriously, gentlemen, this is no publicity stunt. The dog has actually vanished. He hasn't been seen on the post since you men were here yesterday."

"You wouldn't kid us, Lieutenant?" The reporter at the pillar was still doing the talking. "Sure you didn't hide him yesterday and forget where you put him? Think hard, now."

"I give you my word as an officer that I haven't the least idea of where he is. I wish I did. Seriously, we are very much concerned about it. Rags is a favorite with the general, the big chief in Washington, and what will he think if this post has let something happen to him?"

Convinced at last, the reporters snapped alert.

"Where's a phone?" they demanded in chorus. "This is a swell story. Suppose some one stole him? Maybe a hit-run driver got him."

They raced for telephone booths and poured the news of Rags's disappearance into the ears of their editors. In spite of the competition of Wall Street and other activities, it was news. "Rags A. W. O. L." was the way most of the papers played it.

A few hours later the lieutenant who had lost the bet on the return of the news men strolled into the officers' quarters.

"Darned little terrier's smarter than I thought," he commented. "He sure picked the right time to disappear."

"Don't you think he's really lost?" another officer asked.

"Of course not. Where would he get lost? He never goes off the post on account of the automobiles. The little fox is hiding out somewhere— probably laughing in his whiskers."

A telephone jingled. The club steward answered it.

"Headquarters on the wire," he announced. "Wishes to speak to the ranking officer."

A tall captain unwound himself from an armchair and went to the phone. The conversation was brief. He returned to the lounge.

"It seems our good friend the loot, here, is slightly in error," he announced. "Rags is actually missing, A. W. O. L., vamoosed, non est, all gone. And the little soldier boys will please bestir themselves and find him. And until he's found said soldier boys, including the commissioned personnel, will cancel all social and other engagements and join the posse commitatus. Fall in. Cherio. Report at division after dinner."

He sat down with a sigh.

"And I had a date with my very best, bestest girlfriend tonight, too," he murmured. "Rags, how could you?"

"You mean Division has taken official cognizance of the fact that Rags is missing?" cut in the bet-losing lieutenant.

"Not only division, old dear, but corps. In other words the whole blessed army in this area. Only that and nothing more."

"Looks like he's actually lost, then."

"It certainly does. Lost, which I doubt; strayed, which isn't like him; or stolen, which seems most probable."

CHAPTER TWENTY
A VETERAN'S LAST CHARGE

WHEN Rags reached the dock after his abrupt departure from the parade-ground, several boats were there, including the launch he had first seen when he was at Governors Island. They had transported soldiers from the island for the rehearsal, and were waiting to take them back. The terrier scrambled aboard the launch. A soldier noticed him and spoke to a sergeant.

"Here's Rags," he announced. "Looks like he wants to go joy-riding."

"He can't," the sergeant ruled. "They want him here for the reunion. Set him ashore."

"Aw, let him come. We can bring him back tomorrow."

"Nothin' doin'. He's one o' the stars o' this show. The generals are all hot and bothered about it, as it is. If Rags was missin' they'd make the place blue. I don't want no general tyin' knots in my tail. Put him ashore."

The soldier grumblingly obeyed. Rags, unused to such treatment, boarded again. Once more he was put off. He stood for a moment, eyeing the men with a puzzled air. Then he moved down the dock. He inspected a mine-planter carefully. Seeing no sign of life on it, he scrambled aboard and hid among some coils of rope and cable. There he remained until the craft moved out, carrying the men of the Sixteenth Infantry back to Governors Island. At the island he waited until the troops had debarked and the boat appeared deserted. Dusk was just blending into night. The terrier stole quietly ashore and by a circuitous route made his way to the quarters of his old friend, the stable sergeant. He scratched several times and barked guardedly before the door opened.

"Hello yourself!" the sergeant cried in surprise. "How'd you get here, and why?"

Rags barked, wagged his tail, and lay down under the sergeant's cot.

"Fixin" to stay awhile, eh? Wonder if you've had your dinner. Guess I'll rustle you some grub, anyhow."

Rags was hungry and attacked the food with energy. MacGregor drifted in. He looked at the terrier in surprise. Then he laughed.

"Just what you'd expect of the smart little pup," he remarked, and recounted Rags's narrow escape from the automobile in the afternoon.

"He hates automobiles," MacGregor continued, "and he knows darned well they have no business on the parade-ground. He won't stick around with an outfit that's so unsoldierly as to let 'em get there."

"So far as I'm concerned," the stable sergeant put in, "he can stay here until he gets ready to go back. An' if he never wants to go back it'll be too soon."

"They'll probably turn the place inside out, lookin' for him."

"Let 'em. I ain't forgot how those jaspers gave us the razzberry when Rags went over there a few years back. Let 'em sweat."

"Suppose they start an official search?"

"Not likely."

"It sure is. Rags stands ace high, with the big chief, who's comin' down from Washington for the review. Those birds don't want to have to tell him: 'Sorry, General, but we mislaid the division's mascot!' Bet you they go over Hamilton an' this place with a fine-tooth comb."

"Maybe. I'll play safe, anyhow."

"What you goin' to do?"

"I'll take him down to Wadsworth. They won't figure him gettin' that far. I got to go over there in the mornin', anyhow."

Bright and early next day, with Rags in a large covered basket, the stable sergeant journeyed to Fort Wadsworth on Staten Island. He explained the situation to an old crony, also a sergeant, and left Rags in the man's care. He was delivering the terrier at about the time the lieutenant at Fort Hamilton was frantically paging Rags. When the general search order came out that night the stable sergeant chuckled.

"Bill won't let loose of him," he confided to MacGregor. "He don't love the Hamilton crowd. They got a guy over there that busted him once—back in the islands. A gugu gave Bill some lip an' Bill kissed him—with the butt of a Krag. Bill was set down for stirring hostility among the natives an' he's had it in for the guy that broke him ever since."

"If they stir up enough fuss he may have to."

"Guess again. If they make it high, heavy, an' official he won't dare to. He'll have to hang on to the dog to cover himself."

Next morning both MacGregor and the stable sergeant realized that the search for Rags had become "high, heavy, and official." Every newspaper in the metropolitan area carried his picture under the apt caption "A. W. O. L." The police had been asked to keep an eye out for him. Nor was that all. Friends of the First Division offered rewards. Candidates for office saw a chance to make a bid for the veteran vote and promptly chipped in—fifty, a hundred, two hundred dollars. The third day after Rags's disappearance from Fort Hamilton the rewards offered for his return aggregated thirty-two hundred and fifty dollars—no mean sum for a small dog of uncertain pedigree. By the fourth day the finder of Rags could have collected forty-four hundred dollars, pledged by more than fifty persons. The stable sergeant, worried, found an excuse to make a hurried trip to Fort Wadsworth.

"Gosh! Bill," he apologized. "I didn't mean to let you in for anything like this. What'll we do? The whole town's gone crazy over this thing."

"What can we do?" growled Bill. "If I turn him in an' take the reward, I'll be a burglar. If I don't take it I'll be on the carpet. No soldier's turnin' down four grand if he's gettin' it on the level."

"Tell 'em you don't want it; that you're glad to do a good turn for the old outfit. Give 'em one o' those 'loyalty to the service' speeches."

"Listen, Mac! The baby who'd do the investigatin', if I was fool enough to try that, is the adjutant. There's a lot of officers you can sell boloney to, but he ain't one of 'em. Try to tell him that a soldier who found Rags on the level would turn down about nine years' pay. Just try it!"

"Well, then, why don't you just turn him loose. Let him show up with no questions asked."

"Yeah. An' have some rookie, with the hayseed still in his hair, find him and grab off the jack. Nothin' doin'. Rags is boardin' with me until this blows over. Then I'll sneak him home some dark night an' leave him on his own doorstep."

As another day rolled around Rags became restless. The sergeant did not permit him to leave his quarters, and when visitors came he tucked the dog into the basket and hid it away. Several times when the terrier attempted to go out the sergeant seized him and gently but firmly dragged him inside. Rags became sulky and refused to eat.

"I'm sorry, old-timer," the sergeant told him. "I don't like to have you feel you're gettin' a raw deal. But there ain't no help for it just now. I got to protect myself—an' I ain't lettin' no rookie get rich on you."

Rags lay motionless, his good eye following every move of his jailor. He assumed an attitude of resignation. Had the sergeant observed him more closely, he would have noticed that Rags was studying the various exits of the place, that his eye frequently rested on a small window, some five feet above the floor. It swung on hinges and usually was open for ventilation. Rags's best leap missed it by about six inches. He had tried, when the sergeant stepped out once, without putting him in the basket.

Directly under it was the sergeant's locker-trunk. But that was too close to the wall to be of use for a leap through the window. Rags had tried it, too.

The division reunion opened without Rags. Veterans missed him, and inquired for him. The people at Fort Hamilton grew glum and blue. They wondered what General Summerall would say when he arrived and found no Rags. Efforts to locate the dog, or at least to learn what had happened to him, were redoubled. But the big day—the review, presentation of battle streamers, and sham battle—came without any news of the missing mascot.

That morning Rags was awake before daybreak. When the sergeant turned out, the terrier watched him narrowly. The man stepped before his locker-trunk and bent down to pick up the clothing he had carefully piled on it the night before. In a flash Rags bounded on his back, and from his back through the open window. Before the sergeant realized what had happened Rags was tearing across the reservation, toward where his nose told him the waterfront lay. There was a small launch tied to the dock, bobbing idly with the play of the waves. Rags started to go aboard, hesitated, then ran back and concealed himself in some shrubbery. Presently a couple of soldiers appeared. Rags watched them from his cover, but made no move.

The soldiers were discussing him.

"What do you suppose became o' that dog?" the taller of the two inquired.

"Dunno. Wish I did. With that reward a guy could go into the banking business in this man's army and clean up, in about three hitches."

"Lady Luck never would put anything like that where I could grab it."

"You an' me both."

The tall soldier glanced at his wristwatch. "Five minutes to six. The cap'n's due at six—an' he'll be here on the dot."

"You said it. Guess we better give this swamp taxi a spin an' see if she'll run."

The soldier swung the flywheel. The motor coughed, and remained dead. The shorter of the two stripped off his blouse and spun the wheel rapidly. Still no response from the motor. Again and again he cranked. Same result.

"Whew!" he gasped, wiping the sweat from his forehead. "If that thing had a mainspring it'd run about ten miles on that last winding. Well, here goes again."

125

Another back-breaking spinning and the motor coughed, hesitated, and then settled into a steady roar. The taller soldier again consulted his watch. It lacked a minute of six.

"Here he comes, right on the line as usual," he told the other, nodding toward a tall, uniformed figure striding down the path about a hundred yards away. Rags also saw the approaching officer, and recognized him as an old friend. With a yelp he tore out of his cover and dashed to meet him. The officer halted in surprise. The soldiers gazed at one another open-mouthed.

"There goes four thousand beautiful simoleons!" the taller observed, sadly.

"Who'll get it, the cap'n?"

"'Course not. Officers can't take that kind o' jack. He wouldn't, anyhow."

"An" the darned little pooch was right under our noses all the time we were talkin' about him."

"We just wasn't born lucky."

"Right. If we'd been lucky we'd o' known the dog an' he'd of come to us. He knows the cap'n, see!"

The officer was talking to the terrier.

"Good morning, Rags," he said, cheerfully. "I hear you've been A. W. O. L."

Rags leaped and barked and seemed likely to wag his tail off. Then he stood still while the officer scratched his neck and back and patted his head.

"I suppose," the captain continued, "you're surrendering at the nearest post, and requesting transportation back to your regular station—in accordance with the regulations?"

Rags listened attentively. He liked having speeches made to him.

"Well, boy, you're in luck. There's an order out to do just that. You've made a lot of trouble, young fellow. What was the big idea?"

"Brup," said Rags.

"Oh, that was it, was it? Well, if it was up to me I'd give you about a month's K. P."

"Brup! Brup!"

"Don't mind that, eh! Come to think of it, K. P. is one of your favorite pastimes. I ought to put you under arrest."

"Brup! B-r-r-up! Brup-er-up-er-up!"

"Oh, it wasn't your fault. I've heard that one before too, Rags. Here we are. Pile in."

He had been walking rapidly as he talked, with the terrier running beside him, or bounding up and down in front of him. He lifted the dog into the boat and followed. Noting the glum faces of the two soldiers, he inquired:

"What's the matter? Sick?"

"And how, sir," the taller answered with a sheepish grin.

"Why didn't you report at my quarters, then? Can't relieve you now. I'm due at Hamilton at nine o'clock and I've got to stop at Governors Island. Just about make it."

"It ain't sick-call sickness, sir," the soldier explained. "We both just got an awful shock, that's all."

"Yeah?"

"The dog, sir. He was hidin' under that bush while we was windin' up the boat. An' we never tumbled to him. Just saw four thousand dollars run down the path, an' never even say goodbye to us."

"Cheer up, boy," the captain laughed. "You're not out a nickel."

"But the reward was offered, sir."

"Certainly. And all of it was offered by civilians. You don't suppose the army would let one of its people take a civilian reward for finding its own lost dog, do you?"

"There would have been an order against it, sir?"

"Why of course! Cheer up."

The soldiers brightened visibly as the launch shoved out into the Narrows and headed for Fort Jay, at Governors Island. There the captain went ashore, spread the news that Rags had been found, and attended to his business. It was a few minutes after nine o'clock when he returned to the launch.

"Step on it," he ordered. "We're late."

The launch sped away from the dock at top speed, the soldiers nursing the engine, to get all the power it had. As the craft drifted into the Fort Hamilton dock the rattle of gun-fire reached them. The small-arms clatter was punctuated, now and then, by the boom of field ordnance. A puff of wind swept the smell of powder gas into their faces.

"Late," the captain grumbled. "The sham battle's on. I wanted to see it, too."

Rags sniffed, cocked his good ear toward the sounds, and glanced inquiringly at the captain. The officer leaped ashore. Rags followed. Without waiting for his companion the terrier broke into a lope, in the direction whence the firing came. The officer was compelled to run to keep up. It was a long drill from the dock to the parade-ground. The

127

captain was getting winded. With an extra burst of speed he overtook Rags and seized his collar.

"Why the mad rush?" he demanded. "Think I'm Nurmi? I'll just fit you out with a set of brakes."

By tying his handkerchief through the loop in his riding-crop and then to Rags's collar, he improvised a leash.

"Now, boy," he admonished, "we'll arrive at the scene "of action with a little of our wind left."

The makeshift leash forced Rags to slacken his pace to match the officer's rapid stride. But, when they came in sight of the parade-ground the terrier began to strain impatiently for freedom. The place was redolent of battle. Army engineers had remade the terrain to simulate a section of World War battle front—and it happened they had selected a section Rags had fought over. At the far end of the setting were the enemy trenches—barbed wire, camouflage, and all the trimmings. In front of them, set precisely from war maps, were hidden machine-gun nests.

Advancing in waves—wearing tin hats and carrying packs—were the troops representing the American doughboys. In the trenches, other regular army soldiers played the part of the enemy. They had the coal-scuttle helmets, but the rest of the enemy uniform had not been available. So they wore their own. It didn't matter, because only the tops of their heads were visible to the three or four thousand spectators. Behind both lines, field artillery boomed. Smoke bombs, scattered over the field, and set off by time fuses, gave the illusion of shell bursts. Here and there men in the advancing waves, simulating casualties, stumbled, fell, and lay still. It was all quite realistic. Rags appeared to take it at its face value.

"When the terrier reached the edge of the parade-ground the captain turned him loose. Rags surveyed the scene for a moment and then dashed to the side of the foremost soldier on the left flank. Hugging the ground closely, he crept forward, timing his pace to that of the man beside him. His entrance into the show gave the officer who was directing it something of a shock.

"Hang it!" he complained, "that darned dog sets the post half crazy by disappearing when he was wanted most; now he gets back just in time to put the show on the blink."

He was about to order a soldier to go and "take that darned dog out o' there," when a limping First Division veteran, long gone civilian, nudged him in the ribs.

"Don't be so hot and bothered," the veteran advised. "Rags ain't hurtin' the show. He's makin' it. He was a member of the original company. Bet you he's the first through the wire."

Another veteran chimed in: "It's kinda tough on those kids, puttin' on this show in the presence of the all-star cast that created the roles."

"They've got the big star with "em," shot back the first speaker. "'Member how Rags crawled through that wire and started bitin' our playmates?"

"Sure do. I noticed my old top kick back there, pinch hittin' as enemy. I hope Rags bites him."

The major listened, hesitated, and decided to let Rags play out the act. The advance was getting closer now. Smoke bombs kept popping behind it to represent an interdiction barrage. Wire-cutters were crawling close to the enemy trench. There was a "twang" at intervals as the tightly stretched wires parted. An officer jumped to his feet. The rush for the trench was on. Rags bounded ahead and was the first through the wire. With a low growl he hurdled the parapet, landing atop the helmet of a squatting soldier. He balanced himself a moment, slipped to the ground and turned, teeth bared, to attack something. Pausing suddenly, as if remembering something, he set himself ready for a spring. He had not forgotten that enemy boots were thick. Then a burst of good-natured laughter brought him out of his fighting trance.

He shook himself as if awakening and looked around. Then he sniffed. The soldiers clustered around him, scratched his back, and patted him.

"Great work," they told him. "You're one swell little soldier yet."

The terrier did not make his usual response. He stood like a statue, tail as stiff as if cast in bronze. From one soldier to another he turned his gaze inquiringly.

"What ails him, do you suppose?" several soldiers chorused.

"Ay tank," said Sergeant Olson, "he vunders vare das enemy bain gone, an' vy ve stand here vile he bain going."

The captain who had brought Rags from Wadsworth strolled along the trench parapet and called to the dog.

"What's the matter, boy?" he inquired. "Pretty tame battle, wasn't it? It's all over. Might as well call it a day. Pass him out, one of you men."

A soldier lifted Rags out of the trench. The terrier looked first at the captain, then glanced over the ground that had been the battlefield a few minutes before. Men were still lying where they had fallen. Suddenly a whistle blew. The "dead and wounded" came to life, jumped to their feet, and walked off the field. Rags focused his good eye on the captain for a moment and then, with a puzzled air, turned away, without bark or tail wave, and trotted toward home. When the family arrived they found him waiting for them on the porch, still looking meditative, and puzzled.

EPILOGUE

AS these lines are written, in the Year of Our Lord 1930, Rags is basking in the twilight of his life, taking his ease as befits an aging veteran. Still hale and hearty, he appears conscious of the dignity expected of his years and rarely displays the frolicsome agility of the old days. He has become more the philosopher, less the dog of action—although he has lost none of his youthful intolerance of cats. Rags still gives the feline population of Fort Hamilton enough exercise to preserve their kittenish figures. But he no longer hunts them with his old-time gusto. His pursuit is perfunctory—a sort of routine matter, attended to out of principle. His zest for exploring has waned, too. He has the fondness for his own fireside so characteristic of elderly folk who have lived full lives.

Occasionally, when the family is away for the day, he will yield to the urgings of some old friend to visit Governors Island, or Wadsworth, or some of the other posts within easy reach of Hamilton. But as the dinner hour draws near his restlessness informs his hosts plainly, "I want to go home." He has given up dining out, almost entirely. He is living out his days quietly, serenely, unconscious of his fame. Not so his family.

Constantly they receive letters inquiring about him; asking about his health; requesting photographs of him. And frequently there are letters containing checks. The writers want to buy some little gift for Rags—a blanket, a collar, or some gadget that the writers think might please him. He wouldn't wear a blanket, he has a collar, and he abhors gadgets of all sorts. The major is put to quite a bit of bother, returning the checks to the donors. The members of the division—and the major—appreciate the spirit behind the gifts; but they have a hard time getting the public to understand that the soldiers would as soon let outsiders buy collars and blankets for General Pershing as for Rags.

Despite his increasing fondness for a quiet existence, Rags attends to his daily exercise with the meticulous regularity of an old soldier. There are perhaps a dozen other dogs on the post, and with all of them Rags has made friends. They appear to have elected him leader of the gang. Almost any afternoon the pack may be seen circling the Fort Hamilton reservation at an easy lope, and in a rough sort of formation, with Rags invariably a few paces in the lead.

If one is lucky and catches Rags near the flag-pole just at retreat, as the flag is lowered and soldiers stand at salute, they may see the little soldier-dog, at stiff attention, saluting too.

131

Growing old, surrounded by his friends, but still alert and active, Rags already is becoming legend; a symbol of canine heroism. He repaid the kindness of the soldiers—with heavy interest.

But it is not unpleasant to recall that, although living only from day to day, with a "rendezvous with death" behind every sunrise, the war-worn soldiers of the First Division had room in their hearts for kindness to a homeless little dog.

THE END

POSTSCRIPT FOR 2005 EDITION

On March 22, 1936 word was received at Fort Hamilton that Rags had died in Washington at the ripe old age of 20. Rags's grave is in Silver Spring, Maryland, at the Aspen Hill Memorial Park Pet Cemetery.

RAGS – R.I.P

THEY SAT HIM ON A BIG CANNON BALL

IF YOU'RE GOING TO SHOOT THAT THING, SHOOT IT

TRAINING FOR THE DOG SHOW

RAGS POSES WITH GENERAL DRUM

RAGS ENTERTAINS AN ADMIRER

OTHER BOOKS YOU MAY LIKE

ONLY A DOG
The True Story Devotion of a Dog's Devotion to His Master in WW1
Bertha Whitridge Smith, ISBN 1905363079
As touching a tale as Greyfriars Bobby!
The true story of a terrier's faithfulness to his soldier master.

CAPTAIN LOXLEY'S LITTLE DOG
Anon, ISBN 1905363133
The dog who refused to leave his master's side for the safety
of a lifeboat when his master's ship was torpedoed in 1915

NURSE AT THE TRENCHES
Letters Home from a WW1 Nurse
Agnes Warner, ISBN 0951565567
Hurriedly penned amidst the incessant roar of mighty guns and surrounded by the
dying, written by a Red Cross Nurse shivering with cold and wearied almost to the
point of exhaustion from working every day from 5.30am to 9pm, these letters give
a fascinating glimpse into the life of a nurse at war.

PLUS MANY MORE!

MOST OF THESE TITLES CAN BE ORDERED FROM ANY GOOD
BOOKSTORE AND WWW.AMAZON.COM

THEY CAN ALSO BE ORDERED FROM US DIRECT AT
WWW.DIGGORYPRESS.COM

Printed in the United Kingdom
by Lightning Source UK Ltd.
109557UKS00001B/216